AF479140

a Brush with the Blues

26 portraits by Jack Coughlin
with commentary by Steven C. Tracy

REP HOUSE LLC

Contents

the artist

Jack Coughlin was born in Greenwich, Connecticut in 1932. He attended the Arts Students League in New York City and then the Rhode Island School of Design, where he received his B.F.A. in 1954 and his M.F.A. in 1961. From 1961 till 1995 he was Professor of Art at the University of Massachusetts, Amherst, Massachusetts. His work hangs in many important public and private collections including the Metropolitan Museum of Art, The Modern Museum of Art in New York City, The National Collection Of Fine Art in Washington, DC, The Norfolk Museum of Arts and Sciences in Virginia, and The Worcester Art Museum, as well as several important museums abroad. He has had one-artist shows at the University of Pittsburgh, Pittsburgh, Pennsylvania, the David Hendriks Gallery, Dublin, the Ainsworth Gallery in Boston, Massachusetts, Harvard University, Cambridge, Massachusetts, and Associated American Artists, New York City to name just a few.

Some of his awards include the *John Taylor Arms Memorial Prize*, National Academy of Design, New York City; *Madison Award for Etching*, Society of American Graphic Artists Exhibition, New York City; *New Jersey State Museum of Art Prize for Etching*, Hunterton Art Center, Clinton, NJ; *Award for Printing*, Purdue University, Lafayette, Indiana.; *Helen Loggie Prize for Drawing*, National Academy of Design, New York City.

He is a regular contributor of drawings to *The New Republic*, and other illustrations have appeared in numerous books including, *Twelve Birds,* University of Massachusetts Press; Austin Clarke, *Mnemsyne in Dust*, Dolmen Press; Robert Francis, *Six Poems by Robert Francis*, Sawmill Press; his own *Grotesques, Twenty Untitled Etchings*, Aquarius Press; *Thirteen Irish Writers on Ireland*, David R. Godine, Publisher.

His body of work includes many mediums including watercolors, lithography, etching, and sculpture. He was elected an Associate Member of the National Academy of Design, New York City in 1977 and is now a full member.

the author

Steven C. Tracy, assistant professor of Afro-American Studies at the University of Massachusetts at Amherst, is the author of *Langston Hughes and the Blues* and *Going to Cincinnati: A History of the Blues in the Queen City* (University of Illinois Press)—the latter winner of the ARSC Award for best published research in jazz, blues, and gospel in 1994—and numerous articles dealing with literature and folklore published in scholarly journals as well as in blues magazines such as *Blues Unlimited, Living Blues, Block,* and *Jefferson.* A blues DJ for fifteen years, a record producer, and author of CD liner notes for a variety of labels, Tracy is also a singer/harmonica player/composer who has appeared on the *Tonight Show* and recorded with his band, The Crawling Kingsnakes (Blue Shadow CD 4707), and with Albert Washington, Big Joe Duskin, Pigmeat Jarrett, and the Cincinnati Symphony Orchestra. Tracy has opened for Muddy Waters, Sonny Terry and Brownie McGhee, James Cotton, B.B.King, Albert King, and many other blues acts, and toured the Netherlands with his band in 1990.

Introduction

African-American

What we are talking about here begins here. Not just African—blues music did not originate or develop on African soil. Not just American—before the colonial North American slave trade began in 1526, there was no music like the blues on these shores either.

African American

And it begins not in a *static* place, but in a nexus, a locus of energy, a place of violence, and turmoil, and confrontation, and sacrifice, and restlessness, and frustration, and accommodation, and perseverence, and creativity, and enrichment, and transcendence; a place where the plantation ledgers and bills of sale of the architects of this country's political and social systems were examined and (un)balanced and found wanting; a place perhaps where the highest ideals of this democracy—personal freedom; exaltation of the masses; the embracing of the spirit of the revolutionary moment and improvisatory celebration in the context of a comfortably loose but securely established structure that welcomes all comers and allows all identities to exist and flourish—are most sweetly and rhythmically exemplified. And yet we must go back to Africa in order to examine who and what it was that existed *there* that was brought *here* to create that which was much greater than the sum of its mechanical parts.

From the primary source of the North American slave trade, the West African savannah region, come the characteristics of African musical performance that have influenced the techniques of African American music over the centuries. We hear the predominance of percussion and percussively played instruments; the antiphonal (call and response) musical and lyric patterns; the vocal and inflectional manipulation, including growling, buzzing, and straining to achieve emotional tension and complexity; the manner of stretching—flattening and inflating—the boundaries of pitches in improvisational and organically decorative fashion, including the flatted thirds and sevenths referred to by some commentators as "blue" notes; the improvisational lyric moments that serve to embrace the immediacy of event, ritual, and artistic moment; the syncopation set up in relation to a metronomic sense that produces a sense of swing and trickster-like willful improvisation weaving in and out of the nodes of regularity; the instruments, particularly of the savannah stringed-instrument tradition, including the kora, halam, and konting (perhaps sources for the banjo), privileged in this country in some ways by the suppression of drumming in the New World; and above all the RHYTHM so dominant in the music, particularly the complex polyrhythmic elements so common in the blues. Furthermore, the figure of the *griot* (also called *jali*), whose important role as music-maker in African societies where Islamic influence and strong chief-based authority is most powerful, is mirrored in some ways in the figure of the blues performer in this country. Witness his function as purveyor of traditional material frequently learned from fathers and uncles but also other male and female community members, and conversely as improvisational innovator extending and renewing that tradition; his status as professional, semi-professional, or amateur musician, sometimes a wandering bard, sometimes a community-based member; his role as singer of songs of praise, history and genealogy, ritual, and gossip and insult—these are ways in which he can resemble the figure of the blues singer, though there are clearly differences as well. The blues singer, for example, is not much of a genealogist, nor an historian describing the ancestral history of a tribal chief's or important person's family, though taken together the blues chart a kind of history in their own way. Altogether, these points drive home an insistent case for survivals of a variety of techniques and situations that produce a music that is similar, not superficially, but modally—the manner of producing and achieving the music is remarkably similar—to African music. And in some ways its communal function is similar as well. We encounter it invoking and producing a spirit that invites involvement and communication both bodily and spiritually, producing unity of performance and sound while acknowledging and affirming counter-rhythmic counter-currents that are nonetheless integrated into the unified whole. And we find the music being used in conjunction with daily activities, and considered a part of daily ritual and meaning, rather than always being separated into an isolated artistic space. But beyond that, there are perhaps subtle ways in which the soul and spirit of African societies inform the ethos of the blues, in ways that are long forgotten, unconscious, and intangible yet just as surely a part of its technical and visceral landscape.

Of course, there is a long musical passage from the first arrival of the slaves in this country and the emergence of the blues, probably sometime in the last two decades of the nineteenth century. It is a passage marked by interludes of reels and square dances, work songs and field hollers, spirituals and jubilees, coon songs and ragtime, ballads and game songs, that preceded and/or existed alongside the blues, living on in the repertoires of songsters and music physicianers out to make a buck and wing on front porch or in back alley, on street corner or in country juke joint. Especially in the work songs—apparently African-derived, secularized group labor songs with their antiphonal structure, highly rhythmic, heavily accented cadences, and improvised or traditional lyrics dealing most frequently with love or hard work and strung together in loosely, frequently emotionally connected units—and the field hollers—themselves similar to work songs but individualized, somewhat freer and more decorative in their vocal lines—we have immediately recognizeable ancestors of the blues vocal style. However, they are still not quite the blues, even if we have examples of blues singers like Texas Alexander, Bessie Tucker, and Son House singing hollers or holler- or work-song-like blues.

It wasn't until, apparently, some time in the 1880s that the form we recognize as the blues first emerged, and it wasn't until 1890 that Gates Thomas collected a lyric in south Texas that was somewhat like the blues, the same year W.C. Handy identifies as the year when he himself first heard the blues. By the turn of the century numerous collectors, folklorists, and performers—Howard Odum and Ma Rainey among them—had noted the presence of the blues among Southern African Americans. Just why the blues emerged at this particular time is hard to say without resorting to mere conjecture and, perhaps, oversimplification. Certainly African American music had been changing generationally, even as it maintained its strong links with the past, but the newest generational shift, which brought to majority the first generation of African Americans born outside of slavery (and hence placed them in a strange yet familiar Reconstruction and post-Reconstruction world for which there was no ancestral experience), may well have been the major socio-political force that made this new blues form and expression necessary, functional, and attractive. When combined with African-derived modalities adapted and transformed on American soil, European-derived strophic/stanzaic lyric organization, and common blues-ballad harmonic accompaniment pattern, there was created the chronological, geographical, musical, and spiritual space in which the blues could be midwifed into existence.

Of course, the earliest "blues singers" appear not to have been singers of only blues but performers and entertainers who drew upon folk sources—ballads, hollers, spirituals, dance tunes, etc.—and popular sources—minstrel songs/coon songs (often themselves folk-derived), ragtime, and popular sheet music. Their performances at country dances, medicine shows, white functions, and on the streets or in back-country juke joints provided a range of functions, from dance accompaniment to social commentary to parody, as is so clearly evident in the works of such performers as Henry Thomas, Frank Stokes, and Jim Jackson. Clearly the blues was taking its place beside other African American music in the late nineteenth and early twentieth centuries, and it was poised to gain its ascendancy in terms of popular mass consumption with the sheet music publications of Hart Wand's "The Dallas Blues" and W.C. Handy's "The Memphis Blues" (both published in 1912) and the criminally-delayed entry of the African American blues singer into the arena of recorded music.

It was the initiative and drive of Perry Bradford and the reluctant "bravery" of Fred Hager that finally ushered African American blues to the turntable. Pianist-composer-entrepreneur Bradford, who had experienced some success with his *Made In Harlem* revue, initially took two of his compositions ("That Thing Called Love" and "You Can't Keep a Good Man Down") and revue star Mamie Smith to the Victor label, who rejected Smith for fear of alienating their white customers by recording an African American artist. Bradford then moved on to Fred Hager at OKeh, who reluctantly agreed to record the sides by Smith when Hager's first choice, Sophie Tucker, was unavailable. Based on that record's success, Mamie was brought back into the studio on August 10, 1920, to record the first blues record by an African American, "Crazy Blues" and "It's Right Here for You (If You Don't Get it. . . . Tain't No Fault of Mine)"—titles that must have surely also reflected the company's initial hesitance to record and release music by African American artists, as well as the African American press' calls for African American record releases and for the support of the African American public to purchase them. When the record sold 75,000 copies in its first month of release, convincing record companies of the commercial viability of such a product, the craze for female vaudeville blues singers was on.

These vaudeville blues, though, were different from the "folk" blues that African Americans had been singing and folklorists had been collecting in the rural South. Those folk blues were frequently performed by non-professional, sometimes itinerant, musicians in informal situations that allowed for great flexibility or informality in the musical and lyric structure of the song while still observing certain general traditional structural guidelines. The most common musical structure sauntered somewhat in the direction of twelve bars or measures, employing a I-IV-V chord pattern and utilizing a variety of lyric patterns, several sometimes used side by side in the same song: one "line" or thought repeated in roughly the same language three times (AAA); one line repeated twice and then answered or completed or somehow resolved by a third, rhyming, line (AAB); one line sung and then completed by a rhyming line repeated twice (ABB); and one line sung, followed by a different rhyming line, leading to a refrain that carries over from stanza to stanza (AB refrain) being the most common twelve-bar patterns. Many of the thoughts termed "lines" might actually be heard or transcribed as two "lines" since a strong medial caesura is frequently characteristic in the vocal performance of the blues line. In addition to the common twelve-bar patterns, eight-bar patterns were common in the tradition as well, featuring a variety of lyric patterns (AB; AB refrain). Unfettered by the length limitations of the 78 RPM record, performances could and would frequently exceed their roughly three minute length, and could be more loosely and associationally—and occasionally—constructed than the blues recorded in the studio for popular consumption, which themselves tended to develop over the years toward more tightly and/or logically plotted story lines or themes. Folk blues were performed with a specific audience present and in mind, and with an expectation of immediate feedback, and the character of the songs frequently depended in part upon the audience for their content, directions, and dynamics of performance. Finally, these folk blues included formula-like phrases and lines that were employed by many singers, in a way not exactly identical to but similar to the oral-formulaic usages described by Parry and Lord in their descriptions of oral epic poets. Common lines or phrases such as "Woke up this mornin" or "I'm goin away" were used to set certain ideas or themes in motion in relation to traditional models, in the context of which the singer could generate any number of completions of the traditional language to accomplish his or her individual purpose in the song. Such techniques can give individual songs a simultaneously traditional and individual feel, emphasizing both the communal and personal aspects of blues lyrics.

By contrast, the vaudeville blues that were brought to record by Mamie Smith frequently had a number of characteristics that set them apart from the folk blues. The songs were frequently composed by professional tunesmiths and were thus somewhat stylized, though some vaudeville blues singers did write their own blues and many of their songs did draw in some way on traditional lines and phrases. In addition to the twelve-bar structure, they often also featured introductory lyric or narrative passages or eschewed the twelve-bar structure for 16, 24, or 32-bar structures. The singers themselves were in numerous instances professional stage performers who appeared in revues and stage shows, singing pop songs, dancing, and/or performing comedy skits as well. Their accompanists were frequently trained professional jazz musicians performing somewhat sophisticated arrangements, though improvisation was of course present to varying degrees. And finally, the songs' lengths were crafted to fit on one side of a 78 (though certainly two-sided records were possible, obviously the song would have to start over again for part two, and the intervening time and effort it took to turn over the record surely broke up the performance into two distinct parts rather than providing a continuous whole). These were the first blues produced for popular consumption on record, and for a number of year—and 1923-1926 was their hey-day—singers such as Mamie Smith, Lucille Hegamin, Clara Smith, Victoria Spivey, Rosa Henderson, and the two most outstanding exponents of the genre—Ma Rainey and Bessie Smith—enthralled listeners with their tales of women's woes and triumphs, declaring from the stages of cabarets, theatres, and tent shows their (pop-) blues messages of weariness, frustration, defiance, and liberation. At times, especially in the cases of Ma and Bessie, they declaimed with such power and style that, no matter how pop-influenced the arrangement or lyrics, they struck to the heart of the deepest blues.

In the meantime, male country blues/folk performers continued to entertain across the South, making no inroads in the recording industry until the 1923 guitar solos by Sylvester Weaver and 1924 sides by Reese Du Pree, Daddy Stovepipe, Stovepipe No.1, Papa Charlie Jackson, and Ed Andrews. However, it was the phenomenal success of Blind Lemon Jefferson in 1926 that proved that male country blues artists (and female country blues artists as well) could produce profit for record companies, sending company agents and representatives into the fields in search of country blues talent in a variety of geographical areas. Such forays began to provide a picture of a number of different regional blues style tendencies that were tied in a number of ways to conditions in the geographical location: the source in Africa of slaves brought into that area; the relations and interactions between blacks and whites in the area; the proximity and access to other kinds of music; the popularity and/or dominance of a particular area performer; and the access to commercial blues recordings are among the most important determinants producing regional tendencies—not absolutes. For example, we tend to associate Mississippi Delta blues with insistent, jagged polyrhythms, harsh and raspy vocal timbre, limited melodic range, and unrestrained intensity, all characteristic of Drew/Dockery blues legend Charlie Patton and his "pupils" Son House and Willie Brown. And yet other excellent Mississippi blues performers such as Tommy Johnson, Skip James, Mattie Delaney, and John Hurt lack one or more of these "typical" characteristics. In Texas, reels, play party songs, work songs, and field hollers are very directly prominent in the work of older generation Texas-area performers such as Henry Thomas, Texas Alexander, Bessie Tucker, Rambling Thomas, and King Solomon Hill. Among the younger Texas-area artists of the 1920s and 1930s, a lighter, mid-tempo, ragtime-influenced (but not dynamically flashy) music—with a steady, thumping bass, ornamental and rhythmically free treble part, and voice timbre that was less harsh than the "typical" Mississippi blues singer—prevailed. And yet above it all, similar in some ways and yet gloriously different, was the daunting figure of the virtually uncopyable Blind Lemon Jefferson. In the Southeast states, dazzling guitar technique (polyrhymic syncopated bounce and flashy chords and runs borrowed from ragtime music), smooth vocals, and sometimes boastful, light-hearted, double-entendre lyrics were common, crafted most beautifully by the influential Blind Blake, along with Gary Davis, Willie Walker, and Blind Boy Fuller, with a strong twelve-string guitar contingent including Barbecue Bob and Blind Willie McTell located in and around Atlanta. One could similarly enumerate these types of regional tendencies for such areas as Tennessee and their great jug bands, St. Louis, and Alabama, as well as for blues and boogie woogie piano styles represented by the Thomas family, Roosevelt Sykes, Walter Davis, Albert Ammons, Pete Johnson, and Meade Lux Lewis, and then move on to the great harmonica players, such as Bullet Williams, Jaybird Coleman, Eddie Mapp, Blues Birdhead, and others.

Suffice it to say that there was a broad variety of blues styles, styles that began to coalesce into a smaller number of urban blues styles by drawing on the work of a number of urban blues pioneers of the 1930s and 1940s. There were the smooth, wistful vocals and beautifully integrated instruments of Leroy Carr and Scrapper Blackwell; the suave sophistication and pioneer virtuoso guitar work of the melismatic Lonnie Johnson; the Bluebird beat band blues of Big Bill Broonzy, slide guitar wizard Tampa Red, powerhouse pianist Big Maceo, and harmonica ace Sonny Boy Williamson, each also distinctive vocalists in their own rights, and the Chicago through Memphis hard-bitten fireworks of Memphis Minnie; T-Bone Walker crystallizing the contributions of Blind Lemon, Lonnie Johnson, Scrapper Blackwell, and jazz pioneers Django Reinhardt and Charlie Christian into his own distinctive and influential single-string style; and the shouting of Kansas City's Big Joe Turner, the bluesy crooning of Nat King Cole-inspired Charles Brown, and the gospel and gospel-influenced stylings of Sister Rosetta Tharpe and Dinah Washington. All of these were styles produced and/or influenced by increasing urbanization, greater use of amplification, and wider employment of larger ensembles, leading the metamorphosis of the blues from its rural roots to its varied urban expressions and clearing the way for subsequent blues recording artists from the 1950s to the present: Muddy Waters, Little Walter, and Elmore James in Chicago; Howlin' Wolf, Junior Parker, and Little Milton in Memphis; the T-Bone Walker-influenced guitarists B.B., Albert, and Freddy King, Gatemouth Brown, and Albert Collins; and the rhythm and blues and soul stylings of Big Maybelle, Esther Phillips, Jimmy Reed, Slim Harpo, Professor Longhair, Fats Domino, Wilson Pickett, and so many others, on down to contemporary performers such as Sugar Blue, Robert Cray, and Millie Jackson.

Through it all, the blues singer has provided both a personal and communal voice that encompassed the varied experiences of the African American in a racist society. "The blues started from slavery," Memphis Slim stated authoritatively in a conversation with Big Bill Broonzy and Sonny Boy Williamson, and indeed the blues is imbued with the lash of slavery, the empty promises of Reconstruction, the indignities of Jim Crow, and the continuing inequities inherent in

American society. Blues performers themselves have defined the blues in their own songs—"the blues ain't nothin but a woman lovin a married man," "the blues ain't nothin but a low-down shakin chill," "the blues ain't nothin but a botheration on your mind"—but just as surely as the blues are rooted in these kinds of specific immediate experiences, they also draw upon an historical and emotional backdrop about which B.B.King has commented, "After you have lived in the [Jim Crow] system for so long, then it don't bother you openly, but way back in your mind it bugs you." Blues performers may not, in fact, always be describing solely their own experiences in their songs. Sometimes they spin out narratives of the experience of relatives, friends, neighbors, or other community members, or experiences that any community member *could* have had, or experiences that reflect a symbolic rather than a literal reality, but almost all in the first person, as if the experience had been their own. Some songs like "Just a Dream" by Big Bill Broonzy portray the desire for some condition or circumstance that doesn't exist, like a welcome for a Black man from the President in the White House. But whoever had the actual experiences, by drawing on traditional vocal and performing techniques adapted to and altered based upon the singer's creativity and abilities, by using traditional lyric "formulas" and stanzas transformed to relate to contemporary experiences, and by tapping into characteristics of expression and performance that can be seen as part of a kind of "blues persona"—in these ways blues performers can be seen as purveyors of both personal and communal, contemporary and historical, realities and visions. First person singular on the surface, first person plural down deep, multi-tensed in their echoes of the past, soundings of the present, and reverberations in the future. Unifiers.

Direct, immediate, insinuating, sensual, potent—something foxy and fine, moving on bulldog-hug-a-hound legs that have strutted and sashayed around the block (and across the ocean) enough times to know the blues by rote. Pigmeat built on an old hog frame—twelve sweet measures of humanity large enough to fit us all, but tight like that just the same. Full of mojos and turnrows and power and pain, distilled exquisitely into sweet showers of rain. A creative ritualistic celebration delivering high-born syncopators to the still-promised land. The Blues. These faces, famous and obscure, a random selection of images reflecting only part of a vast tradition, a cherished and loving brush with the blues.

Steven C. Tracy

a Brush with the Blues

Bessie Smith

Bessie. She has first-name recognition, and calling her name is all it takes to find a synonym for the blues. With a voice timbre like a trombone with a hurricane howling through it, impeccable phrasing and clear diction, and a feeling for the blues that seems to well up from the soles of her feet and involve her entire body in tremulous fervor, she has been the standard by which all other female blues singers have been judged, and she still reigns as the Queen, the Empress of the Blues. One of seven children born to part-time preacher William Smith and his wife, Bessie was born on April 15, 1894, in Chattanooga, Tennessee. She began singing on the streets for stray coins after her parents died before she was eight years old, graduating to tent shows as a chorus girl and singer c. 1912. Eventually she joined various revues, such as the Rabbit Foot Minstrels and the Silas Green Minstrel Show, as they traveled throughout the South, where she honed her craft and met Ma Rainey, from whom she may have picked up some suggestions about dealing with the grueling tour conditions, and who may have in fact exposed Bessie to the blues. From there and then on it was Bessie's own rocket that propelled her to fame. After possibly recording a test pressing for Black Swan/Emerson in 1921 and a test for OKeh in 1923, she finally reached people's phonographs in 1923 on Columbia Records, remaining with that label for the rest of her recording career, which ended in 1933. Initially, Bessie worked in plain street clothes, relying strictly on her considerable talent to reach her audience, but over time and with her great commercial appeal, she gradually dressed more elaborately, in a manner more suited to her wild success and celebrity. From her first released recording, "Down Hearted Blues," she demonstrated a command of her voice and material that was so compelling that she was virtually untouchable at her craft, and previous African American pop and vaudeville blues singers began introducing blues with a more down home feeling into their repertoires in response to the gauntlet she had thrown down. In fact, Bessie's recordings exerted a tremendous influence on many jazz and blues performers, who picked up stray lyrics or entire songs, images, and techniques from her widely disseminated records, a moanful "Jail House Blues," W. C. Handy's "St. Louis Blues," "Back Water Blues," "Young Woman Blues," and "Nobody Knows You When You're Down and Out" being among the most memorable. With accompanists like Fletcher Henderson, James P. Johnson, Coleman Hawkins, Don Redman, Charlie Green, Tommy Ladnier, and Louis Armstrong, a lesser singer might have been overwhelmed, but Bessie clearly remained the dominant presence on her recordings, her independent spirit serving notice to all who came to play that she was the focal point, and her strong will and unmatched prowess ensuring a supremely high quality throughout her recording career. Unfortunately, there were complications in her personal life with her husband Jack Gee over various sexual liaisons, but through everything—the personal difficulties, the frequent tours and revues, the recordings, the two-reeler film short—she persevered, recording her last session in 1933 with Benny Goodman, Jack Teagarden, and others, and remained a popular touring attraction until her death on September 26, 1937, of injuries suffered in an automobile accident. Years later, after numerous awards, an acclaimed play by Edward Albee treating her life, and induction into the Blues and Rock and Roll Halls of Fame, it is still one of life's redeeming pleasures to sit and listen to Bessie Smith with just a piano accompanist—her preferred setting—conjure and dispel the blues.

Bessie Smith
Jack Coughlin '98

Ma Rainey

She was the only female blues singer to give Bessie Smith serious competition, and to some, for example Georgia Tom Dorsey, she was "the greatest of the blues singers." When she moaned about bo weevils and screech owls and the cornfield blues, you knew that she'd been there and back, most exultantly back, absorbing and translating her troubles and the troubles of her people into art of abiding beauty; when she sang "Yonder Come the Blues," you could see them, feel them, dragging themselves up over a dusty, hilly, scorched road into her life and yours, and you were glad Ma Rainey was there on the lookout. "The Mother of the Blues" was born Gertrude Pridgett on April 26, 1886, in Columbus, Georgia. Both of her parents, Thomas Pridgett, Sr., and Ella Allen, were minstrel troupers, and young Gertrude sang and danced her way into the business in c. 1900 in *A Bunch of Blackberries* in her hometown. Though not always strictly a blues singer, she was captivated by a blues song she heard sung in 1902, and thereafter included that type of music in her act with increasing frequency. In 1904 she teamed up with husband Will "Pa" Rainey, billed as the Assassinators of the Blues, to tour tent shows and other venues throughout the South and Midwest, occasionally working the same shows as the younger Bessie Smith, who may have picked up a pointer or two from Ma, though their styles were ultimately dissimilar. In 1923 she finally recorded for Paramount Records, accompanied by Lovie Austin's Blues Serenaders, and she remained with that company throughout her recording career of nearly one hundred sides. Roughly half of the songs she recorded were authored or co-authored by Rainey—a significant tribute to her talent and ability—and she demonstrated time and again a deep familiarity with African American folklore, the pitfalls of big city life, and the classic blues theme of the mistreatment at the hands of one's lover, along with a willingness to confront issues of prostitution and homosexuality in a direct, honest fashion. On stage all feathered boas, flash, and flamboyance, she nonetheless could draw at will on her low, unadulterated, mournful contralto to strip back the layers of glitz to the heart of her matter, and on record she employed some of the finest jazz players—Louis Armstrong, Tommy Ladnier, Charlie Green, and Coleman Hawkins—to accompany her in large groups, though she did record with blues artists like Tampa Red and Georgia Tom, Blind Blake, and Papa Charlie Jackson as well. After her final recording session in 1928, she continued to tour until 1935, when she retired to live with her brother and involve herself in the activities of the Friendship Baptist Church and to own and operate the Lyric and Airdome Theatres in Rome and Columbus, Georgia. On December 22, 1939, the future Blues Hall of Famer died of a heart attack, significantly, in her hometown, because she had proved repeatedly on record that she could go home again, and the love she had for home was reflected in the gloriousness of her recordings. Poet Sterling Brown portrayed her in "Ma Rainey" as a prime exemplar of the crucial reciprocal relationship between artist and audience, a caster of marvelous and mysterious, yet familiar, spells: "She jes' catch hold of us, somekindaway." She still has her hold.

"MA" Rainey
Jack Coughlin

Blind Lemon Jefferson

Although he was not the first recorded male country blues performer, Blind Lemon Jefferson successfully initiated the era of country blues recordings and put blues by male blues singers on the map, all the while scaling an aesthetic height that few others could reach. With his high lonesome cottonfield moan soaring mournfully over his nimble, darting, surging guitar, he made record companies take notice of more than blues songs by women who largely made their livings on the stage, bringing street corners, juke joints, and barrelhouses into the living rooms of Race Record buyers with such artistry and power that his name has become synonymous with the poetry, technique, and soul of the blues. Blind Lemon Jefferson was born in 1897 in Couchman, Texas, to farmers Alec Jefferson and Classie Banks. One of seven children, young Lemon was apparently born blind, but he retained some independence by supporting himself as a musician, playing guitar and singing on the streets and at picnics and house parties, led around by various sighted musicians like Leadbelly, T-Bone Walker, Lightnin' Hopkins, and Josh White. He was "discovered" on the streets by pianist Sam Price and taken to talent scout Mayo Williams of Paramount Records in 1925, where in five years he recorded over one hundred sides, with 43 phonograph records issued on 78 RPM. His recordings, featuring his complex, idiosyncratic guitar style (agitated single string treble runs careening into restless antiphonal bass line responses), taut, high-pitched voice, and evocative lyrics, were often commercial successes in the Race Record market, spreading his influence across the country and eventually around the world. Songs associated with Jefferson, such as "Broke and Hungry," "Match Box Blues," and "See That My Grave Is Kept Clean," entered the repertoires of countless musicians lyrically and stylistically, and one can trace the development of the single-string, post-war blues guitar style associated with B.B. King back through T-Bone Walker to Blind Lemon, Lonnie Johnson, and Scrapper Blackwell. Sometimes venerated as an archetypal blues singer—blind, itinerant, and passionately poetic and creative—he influenced the work of Lightnin' Hopkins, Howlin' Wolf, Albert King, B.B. King, Leadbelly, Brownie McGhee, Jimmie Rodgers, Tom Shaw, T-Bone Walker, Josh White, Hop Wilson, Canned Heat, Jefferson Airplane and countless other artists, though his style has rarely been successfully copied, even by the most accomplished guitar technicians or the most soulful stylists. Ultimately, it is difficult to imagine what the legacy of recorded blues might be like without him. He died in Chicago in December, 1929, under mysterious circumstances, freezing to death alone in the snow as he returned from playing a house party, having helped transform the blues recording market and leaving behind a body of work that is among the treasures of American music. Blind he may have been, but the vision he supplied of the blues, and for the blues, demonstrates that he saw clearly what the blues, and life, are all about.

Blind Lemon Jefferson

Big Bill Broonzy

He could be anything anybody wanted him to be, from plaintive country bluesman to fingers-flying ragtime guitarist to sly hokum teaser to tough urban blues belter to charming, sage folk performer and balladeer—but whatever he was, he was always and only distinctively himself, simply one of the most irreplaceable performers in the history of the blues: Big Bill Broonzy. William Lee Conley Broonzy was born on June 26, 1893, in Scott, Mississippi, one of 17 children born to ex-slaves Frank Broonzy and Mittie Belcher. A farm hand in Pine Bluff, Arkansas, in his childhood, young Bill learned to play fiddle from his uncle Jerry Belcher, subsequently working as a fiddler (and preacher) in Arkansas and after he moved to Chicago in 1920. Somewhere in the 1920s Broonzy picked up the guitar and, having mastered it, persuaded a somewhat reluctant J. Mayo Williams of Paramount to record him in a duet with John Thomas in 1927. Between then and 1949, Broonzy recorded some 300 sides as a leader and many more as a popular session man and group member in Chicago for labels like OKeh, Bluebird, ARC, Vocalion, and Columbia. During this time Broonzy was one of the undisputed kings of the blues, combining deep Southern feeling, good-timey swing, sage philosophizing, and astonishing fingerpicking and flatpicking abilities with consummate songwriting skills to produce many classic blues recordings, "Big Bill Blues," "Just a Dream," "Good Liquor Gonna Carry Me Down," and "Long Tall Mama" among them. Appearances at the *From Spirituals to Swing* concerts in 1938-1940 introduced him to white audiences, and later recordings done by Alan Lomax in New York, featuring Broonzy (as Natchez), Memphis Slim, and John Lee "Sonny Boy" Williamson discussing their lives and performing, comprise one of the most amazing and valuable documents of the blues tradition. When the new generation of Chicago blues performers emerged in the late 1940s/early 1950s, a magnanimous Broonzy played the role of encouraging veteran. However, a dividend of his *From Spirituals to Swing* days paid off big when Broonzy was invited to appear in Europe in 1951 and thus began a string of club and concert dates and copious recording sessions in Europe and America (some three hundred more sides!) that lasted until his death. He was marketed at times as the last of the old time blues singers, and Broonzy played that hand superbly, reaching way back to his deepest roots to produce some of his most heartfelt, downhome material, and he could still razzle dazzle with his uptempo work, swing out on folk and pop tunes, and prick peoples' consciences with pointed topical material. Achieving literacy in the 1950s, he saw a selection of his letters describing his life published in 1955 as *Big Bill Blues*, the first published blues autobiography and an important and fascinating work. Even after he was stricken with lung cancer, Broonzy nonetheless continues to perform until he lost his voice, succumbing to cancer on August 15, 1958, in Chicago. The presence of pallbearers Tampa Red, Brother John Sellers, Muddy Waters, Otis Spann, and Sunnyland Slim testifies to his influence and the admiration he inspired among performers of his generation and his younger disciples as well as blues audiences around the world, who saw him inducted into the Blues Hall of Fame.

Big Bill Broonzy   Jack Coughlin

Memphis Minnie

By now the notion of two people being "soul mates," their two hearts beating as one, is a bad cliché, the ludicrous hyperbole of the third-rate novelist—and yet how else to explain the remarkable, intuitive intercourse between Memphis Minnie and Kansas Joe McCoy, whose brilliant guitar duets are the astonishing wedding of unconstrained extemporaneous invention and immediacy with arrangements so tightly and flawlessly executed as to seem the work of one guiding force? Clearly living together, eating the same food, breathing the same air accounts for part of it; immense technical talent, yes; years of hard work and practice shouldn't be discounted. But listen to "I Don't Want That Junk Outa You" or "Let's Go to Town"—*that* is integrated artistry of almost supernatural proportions, artistry so simultaneously relaxed and disciplined that it resembles nothing less than a gangly drunk successfully negotiating a tightrope walk across the Grand Canyon: exhilaratingly unbelievable. The woman who recorded more than 260 recordings in a 30-year recording career spanning 1929-1959, both with and without Kansas Joe, was born Lizzie Douglas on June 3, 1897, in Algiers, Louisana. Growing up in Walls, Mississippi, she felt strongly the lure of nearby Memphis, where, after she had learned to play the guitar by age eleven, she performed with various traveling shows and even teamed up with Delta blues legend Willie Brown. However, it was the team of Lizzie and her second husband Joe McCoy that was discovered on the streets of Memphis by a scout for Columbia Records. She and Kansas Joe produced over 80 sides as a duo for Columbia, Vocalion, Victor, and Decca before they split up in 1935, including aesthetic successes like "Frisco Town," "Meningitis Blues," and the misery-laden "Crazy Cryin' Blues." Minnie's post-Depression, post-Kansas Joe recordings for Decca, Bluebird, Vocalion, ARC, and OKeh were decidedly more urban, though there was a toughness, a raucous edge to Minnie's voice and picking that highlighted and celebrated the downhome core of her music, however much it might be smoothed over by the delightfully swinging piano of Black Bob or Blind John Davis, the sweet steel guitar playing of her first husband Casey Bill Weldon, or the guitar of her third husband, Ernest "Little Son Joe" Lawler (Lawlar/Lawlars). By 1941 Minnie was playing amplified guitar in her urban combo, demonstrating beyond any doubt that she could match any male blues performer note for note in urban blues as she had in her earlier, more rural recordings, and her vocals were even more powerfully assertive in this context. Classic sides such as "Nothing in Rambling," "In My Girlish Days," "Me and My Chauffeur," and "Black Rat Swing," the latter with vocals by Little Son Joe, are among the many highlights of this stage of her career. Stints in Indianapolis, where she owned and operated a blues club with St. Louis Jimmy, in Detroit, and with a vaudeville troupe that toured the South kept her busy in the 1940s, and she continued to perform in Chicago and record for smaller labels like Regal and JOB—along with a session for Chess in 1952—but clearly she was past the heyday of her popularity. She did one final (unissued) recording session in 1959 in Memphis, but her last years found her ill and in nursing homes until she died of a stroke at her sister's home on August 6, 1973, in Memphis, Tennessee. Seven years later, blues fans acknowledged her supremacy by making her among the initial twenty performers inducted into the W.C. Handy Blues Awards Hall of Fame, and she is frequently acknowledged by country blues fans to be at least the vocal peer of Bessie Smith and Ma Rainey and one of bluesdom's top guitarists, as well as a songwriter of great range and skill whose material has been covered by artists as diverse as Bob Wills, Mance Lipscomb, Muddy Waters, and Clifton Chenier. Sadly under-recognized today, she was in her time among the most popular and outstanding performers, with a recorded legacy that will surely endure as long as people acknowledge the blues.

Memphis Minnie

Roosevelt Sykes

Willie Kelly, Easy Papa Johnson, Dobby Bragg, the Honeydripper—whatever you call him, a Roosevelt by any other name is just as sweet an ivory tickler as ever walked the bass of the Earth. Roosevelt Sykes was born on January 31, 1906, in Elmar, Arkansas, moving to St. Louis c.1909 but commuting between St. Louis and West Helena from around 1913, finally settling in West Helena to play in barrelhouses in 1921. Having absorbed the music of "Red Eye Jesse Bell," Sykes went to work with Lee "Pork Chop" Green in Louisiana, from whom he learned the "44 Blues" theme associated with Ernest "44" Johnson and Little Brother Montgomery (as "Vicksburg Blues") but which Sykes was the first to record in 1929. That session came about when Sykes, who had moved back to St. Louis, approached music shop owner and OKeh talent scout Jesse Johnson, who quickly ushered Sykes into a New York studio, beginning a career as a recording artist that stretched over seven decades, included over two dozen labels, and featured accompaniments to over two dozen recording artists as well—including piano on St. Louis Jimmy Oden's original "Goin' Down Slow." During the thirties, Sykes served as a talent scout for Victor even as he continued to tour and play, but he finally settled in Chicago in 1941 to take advantage of performing and recording opportunities. During his career, Sykes recorded everything from deep South moaning blues to bouncing, Wallerish ragtime to smooth ballads to stomp-'em-down to the bricks barrelhouse jive, first working as a solo artist and in duet with Clifford Gibson, then with increasingly larger combos in the 1940s, and then back to a career frequently as a soloist during the Blues Revival. Through it all, his brilliant piano style was remarkably constant: his hands seemed to operate independently of each other: the climbing, lurching, staggering often single-note bass nonetheless integrated beautifully with a prodigious, nervous right hand with a serious mind to ramble, like two separate musicians who intuitively stuck with each other because it was not possible for them to do otherwise—and this was a source of Sykes's ability to translate his style into postwar blues band contexts, because his style had in a sense already forecast it. Coupled with an expressive voice and pragmatic, streetwise, and memorable and creative turns of phrase—Sykes is the author of "Driving Wheel," "Night Time is the Right Time," "Mistake in Life," "The Honey Dripper," "DBA Blues," and "KMA Blues"—and you have one of the blues' most influential and entertaining performers. When the Blues Revival beckoned, Sykes's career was revitalized, bringing him international fame through tours, recordings, appearances in four films, and TV show spots. When he died on July 17, 1983, he was a revered performer and elder statesman of the blues, an influence on major exponents of a variety of blues piano styles—Eddie Boyd, Fats Domino, Henry Gray, Memphis Slim, and Otis Spann among them—and one of the central figures in the transition from rural to urban blues.

Roosevelt Sykes
Jack Coughlin '96

Son House

Death Letter Blues, 1965: churning more furiously than a desperate hurricane, the force seems unimaginable, not only for the brilliant antiphonal guitar interplay of thrashing and resounding snapping, but also the heaving, straining, gutteral roars and whispers that evoke the most frantic nightmares of the dark night of any soul. In his sixties by the time of his "rediscovery," a soft-spoken, shy negro gentleman with a grandfatherly sweet smile beaming atop a meticulously arranged bowtie, he is, in performance, with a National steel guitar grasped in his hands, the enraged and astonished gasp of a battered Job, one of the miracles of the world of art. He was born Eddie James House, Jr. on March 21, 1902, on a plantation between Clarksdale and Lyon, Mississippi, one of at least three children born to Eddie, Sr., a musician in the family brass band. The family moved around Mississippi and ultimately to New Orleans when Son was three or four, and it would be two decades before he would return to Mississippi in his early twenties, a young man who had been preaching sermons in local churches by the time he was fifteen, but a man who was wavering fitfully—and would continue to waver—between the poles of a religious life and a secular one. He began to pick up the rudiments of the guitar c. 1927, captivated first by the bottleneck guitar playing of Willie Wilson and later, after a brief stretch in Parchman State Farm c. 1928-29, with Charlie Patton, who was the premier blues artist in the Mississippi Delta and a strong influence on a host of area blues performers. It was Patton who got Son a contract with Paramount Records in 1930, where Son recorded three two-sided songs that are among the most spellbinding recordings extant—"Dry Spell Blues," "Preaching the Blues," and "My Black Mama"—plus the recently recovered test pressing of "Walking Blues," and perhaps several other unrecovered songs. Son had formed a partnership with vocalist-guitarist Willie Brown before the session, and the two continued to play together in Mississippi throughout the 1930s, when House also worked as a tractor driver, and in the early 1940s, when House was again recorded, this time by Alan Lomax of the Folk Song Archive of the Library of Congress at Lake Cormorant in 1941 and Robinsonville in 1942. The 19 sides House recorded for Lomax are some of the very best recorded by the Library of Congress, featuring an artist whose talents are undiminished from his 1930 sides, playing and singing brilliantly in a variety of settings, from levee camp hollers to solo blues to raucous, four piece band recordings, but always with his trademark impassioned, searing intensity in evidence. The following year, Son moved to Rochester, New York, where he worked as a railroad porter, barbecue chef, and private cook. Separated from Willie Brown, he gradually reduced the amount of time he spent playing until, when Brown died, in 1956 or 1957, Son gave up music altogether. That is, until Dick Waterman, Nick Perls, and Phil Spiro located him and put him on the road to festivals, tours, club dates, and recordings that began in 1964 and continued throughout the early 1970s, including appearances across the United States, in Canada, England, and Switzerland, recordings for Vanguard, Columbia, Verve, Roots, Liberty, and Transatlantic, and spots on TV and in films. He moved to Detroit in 1976 and spent the last years of his life there until his death on October 19, 1988. As a recording artist in his own right and as an influence to blues giants like Robert Johnson and Muddy Waters, Son House is of towering importance in the history of the blues: to watch him transform himself from quiet old man to supernaturally electrified, thrillingly passionate human force is to realize the animating power of the blues, and art itself, to transcend the mundane and generate the eternal out of the common experiences of human existence.

Son House

Billie Holiday

If one defines the blues by the number of bars there are in a stanza, then Billie Holiday recorded few true blues in her lifetime. However, if one conceives of the essence of the blues as residing not in the mechanical or structural, but in the conception of and approach to the lyric and performance, and the communication of an indomitable spirit clashing with overwhelming odds in a battle for independence and self-preservation, then the Lady sure did sing the blues. Born Eleanora Fagan to guitarist Clarence Holiday and Sadie Fagan in Baltimore on April 7, 1915, Billie Holiday's young life was filled with upheaval and hardship. As a child she was passed from relative to relative, wrongfully confined to a home for wayward girls after she was raped, employed as a maid in a whorehouse (remembered fondly as a place where she could listen to records of her two main inspirations, Louis Armstrong and Bessie Smith, and indicative of her roots in the blues), and in 1928 set up a Harlem boardinghouse/brothel where she sometimes worked as a prostitute. However by 1932 she had initiated her singing career at the Log Cabin Club in Harlem, gaining in popularity and ultimately catching the attention of Columbia Records' John Hammond, who appreciated her pulsing, horn-like improvisational skills in a way that some bar owners and patrons did not. She began a nine year recording stint with Columbia, backed at her first session in 1933 by Benny Goodman and his orchestra and subsequently by members of the Teddy Wilson, Count Basie, and Artie Shaw orchestras, among others. After spending 1937 with Basie and 1938 with Shaw, she was invited to accept the plum job at the Cafe Society in New York, increasing her visibility and popularity even more. Among the masterpieces that Holiday produced in the period are "A Fine Romance," "I Can't Give You Anything But Love," "All of Me," "When You're Smiling," "The Man I Love," "God Bless the Child,"

and "Am I Blue," often with brilliant support from Lester Young, Teddy Wilson, Buck Clayton, and Roy Eldridge. In these and her later recordings, Holiday revealed her deeply moving style. Her voice was imbued with the wistful pathos but ultimate perseverance that form the ethos of the blues, a slight catch in her voice hinting at the sob beneath the surface even on her happiest lyrics. And then there is the brilliantly managed tension between the tempo of her accompanists and her own rhythmic phrasing, as if she was trying to resist the world outside herself and establish her own pace and time from within, yet always arriving at the appointed place and time, acknowledging that she was in but not of the restrictive, mechanical, conventional world. And she could swing note for note with the best of her accompanists. Unfortunately, Holiday was becoming increasingly dependent on heroin, going into detox in 1946 and being arrested, convicted, and sent to prison on a drug charge in 1947. Subsequently denied a New York cabaret card, which effectively curtailed her performing career in New York, by 1956, when she was busted for drug possession again, she had added alcohol dependency to her problems. Meanwhile, she continued to tour and record with Capitol, Commodore, Decca, Aladdin, and Verve, sometimes saddled with unsympathetic arrangements or accompanists but contributing frequently stunning performances herself, with a marked increase in raspiness in her voice that effectively made her performances even more world weary and frazzled. She was hospitalized following her final public performance in May 1959, and charged with drug possession while in the hospital, where she died on July 17, 1959, symbolic, perhaps, of the victimization of African Americans and women in this country; but for all the tragedy and exploitation she suffered, she gave back nuggets of the freedom and creativity and beauty she so longed to express unfettered.

Billie Holiday

Blind Boy Fuller

It is difficult to imagine the prewar blues of the Southeastern states without the immensely influential recordings of Blind Boy Fuller, a synthesizer and popularizer whose fine lyric sense and assured, nimble, raggy guitar playing make his 129 separate titles among the most interesting and varied of all blues performers. Born Fulton Allen in Wadesboro, North Carolina, on July 10, 1907, it was not until the time of his marriage to Cora Mae Martin in 1926 that he began to experience serious eye problems that eventually resulted in blindness, and shortly thereafter, made music his primary vocation. Based on the streets of Durham with the assistance of the Welfare Department and consent of the police, Fuller honed his skills and earned his living in the "black bottom" area, ultimately attracting the attention of free-lance ARC scout James Baxter Long, with whom he had a recording agreement, save for a short period with Decca, for the rest of his life. From his first sessions in July 1935 in New York City, it was clear that Fuller had learned well from his teacher, guitar virtuoso and session mate Gary Davis, as well as ragtime-blues guitar master Blind Blake and Carl Martin. Although not the most accomplished or original of artists, he was nonetheless remarkably resilient, a rollicking finger-picker whose zestful enthusiasm positively bubbled over on accelerated tempos ("Step It Up and Go" and "Funny Feeling Blues") and a strong purveyor of sensitive blues lyrics. Fuller reworked popular tunes by Tampa Red in "Truckin' My Blues Away," Memphis Minnie in "Mama, Let Me Lay It on You" and "Flying Airplane Blues," and other well-known blues artists; explored traditional themes like "Crow Jane" in "Untrue Blues;" and even recast an eighteenth-century broadside called "Our Goodman" in his "Cat Man Blues." But he also created interesting lyrics with distinctive images that captured the imaginations of his many listeners and performed outrageously bawdy, double-entendre blues such as "What's That Smells Like Fish" and "Get Your Yas Yas Out." By the time of his death as a result of a bladder infection on February 13, 1941, he had become a commercial enough success to have his music carried on for a short time by Brownie McGhee as "Blind Boy Fuller No. 2," and McGhee and Fuller's harmonica-playing partner Sonny Terry would continue to step it up and go, along with a number of others in North Carolina and on the postwar country blues scene in New York, long after Fuller had stepped it up and gone. Blind Boy Fuller is a member of the Blues Hall of Fame.

Blind Boy Fuller
Jack Coughlin

Sonny Terry

Of all recorded country blues harmonica players, only one has had a recording career spanning nearly a half century of blues, R&B, folk, and rock, frequent exposure on radio, television, in movies, and on the New York stage, gigs from street corners to Carnegie Hall, and a harmonica instruction book publication, and through it all, Sonny Terry retained the magical ability to conjure the barreling locomotives, frenetic yelping of the foxes and hounds, and gut wrenching wails and whoops—the daily sounds—of the rich tradition from which he sprang. Born in Greensboro, North Carolina, on October 24, 1911, the young Saunders Terrell was exposed to the harmonica through the playing of his father, an adept showman, but a man who played no blues. Injuries to first one of Sonny's eyes and then the other at ages 11 and 16 left him with sight in only one eye—and the vision in that one was comparable to looking through a spider web—and caused him to abandon plans to have his own farm in favor of the vocation of musician. Terry met and recorded with Blind Boy Fuller in 1937, but received his big break in the following year when he replaced a jailed Fuller on the bill at John Hammond's 1938 *From Spirituals to Swing* concert at Carnegie Hall. A hit at the show, Terry recorded for the Library of Congress and Columbia Records while in New York and then returned to street corner gigs in Durham. While he continued to back Fuller at his sessions, he also began to record sides as a leader and, following Fuller's death, circumstances eventually threw Terry and guitarist Brownie McGhee into a stormy acquaintanceship and partnership that lasted nearly 40 years and found Terry associating with the likes of Paul Robeson, Woody Guthrie, Pete Seeger, Leadbelly, and the casts of *Finian's Rainbow* (1947-48) and *Cat on a Hot Tin Roof* (1955-1957), in addition to maintaining contacts with New York bluesmen like Big Chief Ellis and Bob Gaddy. Sessions for the Library of Congress, Solo, Asch, Capitol, Savoy, Atlantic, and a host of other labels frequently paired Terry with the smooth voiced and nimble-fingered guitarist McGhee, the perfect foil for Terry's rough-hewn voice and virtuoso harmonica. The pairing was, in fact, inspired, allowing the duo to please the folk crowd with the "older stylings of bygone days" and the R&B crowd with hard-blasting combo blues. Terry, who was adept at singing both in his regular voice and in falsetto, had a sonorous, field-holler-like quality that took many liberties with structure and melody. On harmonica, he was virtually unmatchable on train imitations, fox chases, and "John Henry," and for full-tilt, backwoods wailing, and squabbling, fitful, flashy outbursts, he was the gut-busting king. His death on March 11, 1986, silenced a figure who had through his virtuoso abilities and adaptability spread the gospel of the blues worldwide and brought many people previously unfamiliar with the blues into the fold, earning him a spot in the Blues Hall of Fame. And he was an inspiration to countless musicians, J.C. Burris, Buster Brown, Taj Mahal, Tony Glover, and Johnny Winter among them, though no one save Peg Leg Sam even comes close to matching the down home brilliance of Sonny Terry.

Sonny Terry

John Henry Barbee

One of the benefits of the blues craze in Europe, initiated by the appearence there of Leadbelly in 1949 and Big Bill Broonzy beginning in 1951, was the "rediscovery" and recording of blues performers who had recorded earlier, reactivating worthy, if not always major, artists and giving them the opportunity to show more of what they could do. One such artist was John Henry Barbee, born William George Tucker on November 14, 1905, in Henning, Tennessee. He lived on a farm with his parents, Becker Tucker and Cora Gilton, eventually learning to play the guitar and performing for local suppers and functions in the area until the 1930s. At that time he left home and traveled across the South, working outside of music both as a solo artist and in the company of Sonny Boy Williamson, Big Joe Williams, and Sunnyland Slim in the mid-1930s. After a shooting incident in Arkansas, he assumed the name John Henry Barbee and moved to Chicago, where he finally got the opportunity to record, for Vocalion Records, in 1938. Barbee's five recordings, three unissued at the time, seem to be very much influenced by the blues styles of Memphis in the 1920s and 1930s: he and Willie Bee James create guitar parts that are insistent mixing of chords and single- and dual-string runs, at their best meshing gently but forcefully, and Barbee makes use of both high-pitched and medium-pitched vocal deliveries, demonstrating an attractive voice in various ranges. Particularly effective is his remake of fellow Tennessee musician Allen Shaw's 1934 "I Couldn't Help It," but even the unissued sides, which are occasionally chaotic and untogether, have some fine moments. The recordings, however, did not produce a hit, and after a stint with Moody Jones on Maxwell Street in the early 1940s, Barbee spent some time in the Army and then worked outside of music into the 1960s. By the time he re-emerged in 1963 in concert at the Fickle Pickle and on recordings for Victoria Spivey, he was playing guitar in more of a Chicago boogie style and singing in a lower-pitched and rougher voice, still in a lively, passionate fashion. He was tapped to tour Europe with the American Folk Blues Festival in 1964, recording both live (for Fontana Records) and in the studio (for Storyville Records), but his brief luck ran out when he had to return to the United States due to illness and suffered a heart attack in jail following an auto accident. He died on November 3, 1964, in Chicago, cutting short his "comeback" and depriving the blues world of a solid performer whose honest, straightforward, unpretentious delivery reflected one of the hallmarks of the blues tradition.

John Henry Barbee

Robert Johnson

The legends that have grown up around Robert Johnson, some of them self-created, are frequently so overarching that sometimes it is difficult to get to the essence of the man himself, but recordings like "Hell Hound on My Trail" are so hypnotic, so compelling, located at a crossroads so firmly rooted in the blues tradition yet so revolutionary in pointing toward the future of the music, that it is hard to resist becoming hauntingly awed by the almost mystical power that his recordings exude. Born to Julia Dodds and Noah Johnson on May 8, 1911, in Hazelhurst, Mississippi, Robert Leroy Johnson spent the first few years of his unstable, difficult childhood in migrant labor camps, eventually moving c.1914 to Memphis to live with Julia's husband, Charlie Dodds, Jr. Eventually Julia left her family, but soon an unruly Robert was sent to Robinsonville to live with her. Receiving little schooling, and finally dropping out because of poor eyesight, by the late 1920s Johnson finally picked up the guitar and got some informal pointers from Delta blues legends and patriarchs Willie Brown and Charlie Patton. By a felicitous stroke of luck, one of Johnson's primary influences, Son House, moved to Robinsonville at the behest of Brown, and House held Johnson spellbound with his unrestained, near furious blues, whereupon Johnson set out with great vigor to learn the juke joint lessons House could teach him. Eventually, though, Johnson moved back to Hazelhurst, where he played country suppers and developed not only his skills but a local following as well. A triumphant return to Robinsonville elicited astonishment from Brown and House, amazed at Johnson's progress in a short period of time—Robert Johnson had truly arrived. But Johnson knew he had to leave Hazelhurst for better pickings. He selected Helena, Arkansas, a common stopping-off point for some of the South's best itinerant blues musicians, as his base of operations, though, as he sang in "Walking Blues," he frequently "felt like blowin [his] old lonesome home."

Outside the recording studio Johnson's repertoire included a variety of types of music, including polkas, pop songs, and country music, but it was his blues that were most potent, and Johnson took the initiative in contacting record store owner and sometime ARC talent scout H.C. Speir, who referred Johnson to another scout, Ernie Oertle, who took him into the studio in San Antonio on November 23, 1936, where Johnson recorded eight different songs, returning four days later to record an equal number of sides. Seven months later, Johnson recorded 13 more titles, and then his recording career was over. But what a career it was. His recordings clearly demonstrate the influence of House and other Delta bluesmen, and also reflect his affinity for such artists as Leroy Carr and Lonnie Johnson, but Johnson was able to draw together his disparate influences to create a distinctive style that was smoother and more streamlined, but just as passionate, as House's. Mixing single-note runs, whiney evocations, and sudden bursts of eerie slide to support his high, passionate voice, by turns abjectly mournful and aggressively assertive, he filled his work with startingly poetic lyrics like those in "Hell Hound on My Trail" and "Me and the Devil." Additionally, Johnson employed and helped widely disseminate a distinctive boogie figure in guitar accompaniments to "I Believe I'll Dust My Broom" and "Sweet Home Chicago" that has been frequently copied. Between and after his recording sessions, Johnson traveled extensively with Johnny Shines and Calvin Frazier—as he sang, "I got to keep moving"—but made a fateful return to Greenwood where, having taken up with a married woman, he was poisoned by her husband with strychnine in a juke joint on August 13, 1938, and died three days later, a short time before John Hammond sent Don Law to locate Johnson to play for the 1938 *From Spirituals to Swing* concerts. However, Johnson's legacy lives on in his recordings and his influence on generations of blues artists and rock performers. Johnson altered the direction of blues-based American music, earning himself a central spot in the pantheon of American music and induction into the Blues and Rock and Roll Halls of Fame.

Robert Johnson
Jack Coughlin

John Lee "Sonny Boy" Williamson

John Lee "Sonny Boy" Williamson is a pivotal figure in the history of the blues and the development of the harmonica from its lowly status as a toy to acceptance as an instrument of great range and expressive quality. Born to Ray Williamson and Nancy Utley in Jackson, Mississippi, on March 30, 1914, he began hoboing around Tennessee, Mississippi, and Arkansas in his adolescence, sometimes in the company of Brownsville bluesmen Sleepy John Estes, Yank Rachell, and Hammie Nixon, the latter a harmonica player who was among the first to depart from the set pieces and imitations of performers like Noah Lewis, Bullet Williams, and DeFord Bailey and create a single note, highly vocal style of which Sonny Boy would become the master. Sonny Boy's style employed a brilliant combination of rhythmic, punctuating chords of the older generation (in overdrive) and the exuberant choking, swooping, fluttering single-note magic of the creative genius transforming the techniques of the older players into a contemporary, highly individual expression of the blues of a newer, urban-migration generation. In 1937, three years after he had arrived in Chicago, Sonny Boy commenced a recording career for Victor/Bluebird that generated over 120 sides featuring his enduring, tongue-tied vocal delivery and seminal instrumental style, accompanied by the "Bluebird Beat" session men like Blind John Davis, Joshua Altheimer, and Willie Lacey (whose playing was often galvanized by Sonny Boy), scaling heights not always achieved elsewhere. Add to his performance mastery his skill as a composer—he authored such blues classics as "Good Morning School Girl," "Blue Bird Blues," "Sugar Mama," and a reworking of Walter Roland's "Early in the Morning"—and you have one of the most accomplished and influential entertainers in the history of the blues. Shockingly, Sonny Boy was murdered on June 1, 1948, a robbery victim who was either beaten or stabbed by assailants who apparently didn't know the generous and affable man. Only in his mid-thirties at the time of his death, his influence on the emerging generation of harmonica players like Little Walter, Junior Wells, and Billy Boy Arnold was pervasive, and we can only speculate about what his role might have been in the emerging, heavily-electrified heyday of the Chicago blues of the 1950s and how it would have affected the already electrifying music of the youthful blues legend.

John Lee Williamson

Big Maceo

From the very first tune of his very first recording session, you could tell that there was some special magic taking place: that hickory-smoked, buzzy voice, sensitive, economical piano, and plaintive melody all coalesced into the perfect variant re-creation of Sleepy John Estes' "Someday Baby," placing Big Maceo's "Worried Life Blues" on the roster of classic blues songs and initiating a decade-long recording career featuring some of the most exciting and influential blues piano, and warmest, most tender vocals, in the history of the blues. Born Major Merriweather on March 31, 1905, he was raised by his parents Christopher and Ora on a farm 39 miles west of Atlanta, Georgia. When Major was about 15, the family moved to College Park, Georgia, where he first began to pick up the basics of the piano by hanging around joints on Harvard Avenue. In 1924, Major joined other family members who had migrated to Detroit's East Side, where he worked in the daytime and played house parties at night, eventually marrying Rossell "Hattie Bell" Spruel, who ran one of the houses where he played. Hattie, a shrewd businesswoman, encouraged the unrecorded pianist, now known as Big Maceo (around 6 feet 4 inches, 256 pounds), to travel to Chicago to record, and when Bluebird Beat architect Lester Melrose heard him, he whisked him into the studio to record as leader and as accompanist to Tampa Red, Big Bill Broonzy, and John Lee "Sonny Boy" Williamson. Maceo was the bedrock blues pianist of choice from 1941-1946 in Chicago, eschewing the sophisticated jazz influences that crept into the work of Blind John Davis, Horace Malcolm, Simeon Henry, and others for hard-pounding deep-Delta blues themes, as on "Rambling Mind Blues," with its "rollin' and tumblin'" accompaniment (also employed by Roosevelt Sykes on "Highway 61") and a reworking of the "44 Blues" theme on "32-20 Blues." On uptempo numbers Maceo was particularly powerful: one can only listen with wonder to the breathtaking syncopated virtuosity on songs like "Chicago Breakdown" and "Macy Special," where Maceo beautifully integrates an astonishing array of acrobatic left-hand bass runs with bouncing, trilling, crushing, rolling treble work that recreates the headlong rush of a funky locomotive high-balling it through Chicago towards heaven. Ever versatile, he could also be lightly rollicking on numbers like "Can't You Read," his take on the "Monkey and the Baboon" toast, and wistfully reflective on 8-bar blues such as "Some Sweet Day" and "Things Have Changed." Unfortunately, his career was hampered by a stroke in 1946, which left his right side paralyzed, though he continued recording as a vocalist with Eddie Boyd doing a passable imitation of his piano style on a 1947 session, and Johnny Jones at the piano stool for his Specialty recordings in 1948. By the time of his last recordings for Fortune in 1952, Maceo was playing the left-hand parts on the bass keys while someone else played the treble, but the recordings were not very distinguished. Maceo died on February 26, 1953, leaving for us a treasure trove of classic recordings and a crowd of pianists galvanized by his playing who would draw on his inspiration to develop the role of the piano in the post-war Chicago blues band—Otis Spann, Johnny Jones, Henry Gray, and Eddie Boyd in particular—and to carry on the tradition of blues piano in Detroit, especially Boogie Woogie Red. And even Ray Charles's version of "Worried Life Blues" makes an extended bow towards the old master's style, as if to say that when Maceo did it, it had been done. And so it had.

Big Maceo   Jack Coughlin

Champion Jack Dupree

Drive'em down barrelhouse tickle-stomper, cajoling folk-humorist, social conscience, entertainer extraordinaire, blues ambassador to Europe: each of these designations fits Champion Jack Dupree like the proverbial glove in his chosen arena, the blues. Born to a father of French lineage and a mother of Cherokee descent in New Orleans on July 4, 1910 (ten years to the day after Louis Armstrong), William Thomas Dupree was orphaned at the age of two and sent to the Colored Waifs Home for Boys (where Armstrong also grew up) following the death of his parents in a house fire reputedly set by the KKK. After some rudimentary singing and piano lessons, he ran away from this home at age 14, hanging out around bars and dives where he eventually met pianist "Drive 'Em Down," who helped Dupree develop his pianistic talents. During this time Dupree performed on the backs of trucks with a variety of bands in the French Quarter, Kid Rena's among them, but by his late teens/early twenties he had become a boxer, billing himself as Champion Jack Dupree and working as a pugilist for a decade. A journey North on the Illinois Central Railroad took him, at one point, to Indianapolis, where famed pianist Leroy Carr became a primary influence, Dupree recalling especially Carr's generosity and patience in teaching him "Midnight Hour Blues" shortly before Carr's death in 1935. From his base in Indianapolis, Dupree traveled to perform and MC in Chicago where, spotted by famed scout Lester Melrose in 1940, he was signed and initiated his recording career with OKeh Records. After four sessions in 1940-41 his recording career was interrupted by a call from the Navy, but a session done on leave for Asch kept his fingers nimble until, once discharged and settled in New York in 1945, he set off on a long blues and R&B recording career under a variety of names—including

Willie Jordan, Blind Boy Johnson, Duke Bayou, Brother Blues, Mr. Bear, and Big Tom Collins—for a variety of labels both small—Joe Davis, Continental, Alert, Solo, Abbey—and large—King, Atlantic, and RCA subsidiaries Groove and Vik. From his very first sessions Dupree revealed the influences that would be evident to some extent in his playing for the rest of his life: the infectious, rhythmically insistent bounce of New Orleans barrelhouse piano blended with the economy and wistfulness of Leroy Carr and perhaps Walter Davis and the vocal mannerisms of Peetie Wheatstraw. However, Dupree was no mere copyist: his ebullient personality and wryly humorous outlook on life is reflected in his many recordings from solo outings to larger band sessions. Surely it is hard to imagine a more doomy, bedrock blues session than the one reflected in his *Blues From the Gutter* LP on Atlantic, or a more charmingly humorous series of recordings than those done with Mickey Baker and George Smith for King, which details difficulties of the urban and rural poor with honesty and sympathy, even those that find Dupree walking the perilous tightrope of singing in the voice of a person with a speech impediment. 1960 found Dupree moving to Europe, first Switzerland, then on to Denmark, the UK, and Sweden, remaining there for the final three decades of his life and producing a series of recordings that presented, for the most part, his abilities undiminished and included his reflections on the struggle for dignity and equality in a world that had attempted to deny both to him. When he died on January 21, 1992, having recently made a bit of a comeback in the United States with CD releases on the Bullseye label, he was mourned as a great elder statesman of the blues whose long and distinguished career was his creative and dignified response to the indignities of his existence.

"Champion Jack" Dupree

Memphis Slim

The truly great ones, the ones who have fashioned a style so distinctively compelling that your heart pumps in rhythm in anticipation of their first note, have no fear of telling you where they came from musically because they know they have created their own spiritual and aesthetic home that can be occupied by no other, that is neither above nor below others because it is not about above or below, but alongside, further on down that same road through that same lonesome valley that all artists walk toward that same goal: identity. Memphis Slim is one of the great ones, ever generous in his acknowledgments of his forebears, ever Memphis Slim in his performances. On his Folkways *Greatest Blues Singers* tribute LP he opens, "I'm doing something now that I've always wanted to do—in my own way, of course. This is my own interpretation of some of my favorite blues singers." And he proceeds to pay his respects, in his own way, of course—which is the greatest tribute to the supreme quality of the artists to whom he is paying homage, their perfectly realized individuality. Born John Len Chatman in Memphis, Tennessee, on September 3, 1915, to Baptist deacon/musician Peter, Sr., and Ella Chatman, young Peter absorbed the sounds of the honky tonk next door as a young child, picking out tunes on the piano around age five, playing bass in the school band at Lester High School, and playing music at the Midway Cafe in Memphis before the traveling mood struck him in 1931. From then through 1937 he traveled throughout the South, playing all the dives, juke joints, turpentine camps, and dance halls in need of a deep South barrelhouser to rumble out slow-grind blues and whirlwind boogie woogie. In 1937, he settled his 6 foot 6 inch frame in Chicago, easing onto Big Bill Broonzy's piano stool as replacement for Josh Altheimer and evolving, with Broonzy's encouragement, from a Roosevelt Sykes imitator to a Memphis Slim innovator. By 1940 he was recording with his Washboard Band for OKeh and then for Bluebird in 1940-41, cutting his popular and well-known "Beer Drinking Woman" and establishing himself as a formidable songwriter (a version of "Every Day I Have the Blues" is among his some 300 blues compositions) with urbane delivery and powerful pipes and an authoritative, powerhouse piano style steeped in the sawmill and barrelhouse tradition but perfectly adapted to the emergent urban idiom. Frequent club dates around Chicago in the early 1940s led to recordings for the HyTone label, followed in 1947 by a concert at Town Hall in New York City, after which Slim recorded music and commentary (as Leroy) with Big Bill Broonzy and John Lee "Sonny Boy" Williamson for Alan Lomax. By now Slim was adapting his style even further, this time to combo R&B, most successfully at that point for Miracle and King Records in 1947-1949, producing some of the most wildly infectious boogie woogie grafted onto dual-sax small band riffing on "Pacemaker Boogie," and rolling out slow blues both smooth ("Messing Around with the Blues") and rough ("Grinder Man Blues"). Over the next decade Slim continued to produce blues, boogie woogie, and R&B for a variety of labels, most notably in the company of the House Rockers, featuring guitar wizard Matt Murphy. By the end of the 1950's, though, Slim's days as an R&B star producing sides for Black audiences were nearly over, and he began playing for the new folk/blues audience in America (he received a standing ovation at the 1959 Newport Folk Festival) and Europe, recording a host of LPs for that market. He performed at the American Folk Blues Festival and other club and concert dates, appeared on TV and in films, and eventually took up residency in Europe as yet another blues ambassador, this one at the peak of his powers, a dynamic performer who acquitted himself beautifully as performer and spokesperson for/champion of the blues tradition. In 1978 he was declared Ambassador-at Large of Good Will for the United States by the U.S. Senate, and the French government bestowed upon him the title of Commander of Arts and Letters. Memphis Slim died on February 24, 1988, of kidney failure, in Paris.

Memphis Slim

Willie Dixon

Imagine Muddy Waters without "Hoochie Coochie Man," "Just Make Love to Me," and "You Shook Me," or Little Walter without "My Babe" and "My Baby's Sweeter," Rice Miller without "One Way Out" and "Bring It on Home," or Otis Rush without "I Can't Quit You Baby" or "My Love Will Never Die," Howlin' Wolf without "Spoonful," "Back Door Man," "The Red Rooster," and "Shake for Me," or Wolf and Koko Taylor without "Wang Dang Doodle." Imagine Chess Records without their primary A&R man/producer/talent scout/arranger/session bassist, or the American Folk Blues Festival without its principal impetus, organizer, and rock-solid bassist and vocalist, or the blues rock scene without any of what has been described. Imagine the blues world without Willie Dixon. Born Willie James Dixon on July 1, 1915, in Vicksburg, Mississippi, to Charlie Dixon and Daisy McKenzie, he was raised and worked on a farm for most of his youth, moving to Chicago for good c.1932 and winning the Golden Gloves amateur heavyweight boxing title in 1936. The pugilist turned professional in 1937 but, luckily for the blues world, he also took up the string bass at that time and began working with a succession of vocal groups, from the Ink Spots-inspired Five Breezes, who recorded for Bluebird in 1940, to the Jumps of Jive, Mercury recording artists in 1945, and the Big Three Trio, with whom Dixon recorded from 1946-1949 and 1951-1952 for Bullet and Columbia. The latter group was Dixon's most successful one, laying vocal group harmonies on top of blues songs and arrangements and pointing the way toward R&B groups like the Clovers and the Midnighters. In 1949, though, Dixon began the association that would provide him with the forum for his most influential contributions: he started out accompanying blues artists like Robert Nighthawk for the Aristocrat label, which later became Chicago's premier blues label, Chess Records, with Dixon's able guidance and assistance. Dixon became Chess A&R man in 1952 and was principal architect of the Chicago blues sound in collaboration with the great Chicago blues stars, producing an unprecedented string of hit compositions that have become blues classics, establishing him as one of the most popular and influential songwriters of all time—the songs listed above are only a tiny portion of his many works. Dixon had an uncanny knack for recasting traditional, downhome blues lyrics and ideas into contemporary form and crafting them subtly and carefully for individual artists whose strengths and images he both knew and helped create and solidify. Unfortunately, a monetary dispute caused Dixon to leave Chess for Cobra from 1956-1959, where he produced Otis Rush's classic recordings, but it was his work with Memphis Slim, including recordings for Bluesville, that helped introduce Dixon to the folk and European audiences and initiated the next phase of Dixon's influential career: the blues ambassador/organizer/promoter who brought the blues to previously untapped worldwide audiences through numerous tours and recordings. Dixon hooked back up with Chess in 1960 and continued to tour and record with his own group for the rest of his life, frequently serving as an interpreter of the African-American experience and the blues tradition for new white audiences. His death in Glendale, California, on January 29, 1992, deprived the blues of one of it's greatest exponents and champions, though Dixon's efforts live on through his establishment of the Blues Heaven Foundation, housed in the old Chess building, 2120 South Michigan Avenue, Chicago, Illinois 60616, which promotes the history and reputation of the blues. Willie Dixon is in both the Blues and Rock and Roll Halls of Fame.

Willie Dixon

Howlin' Wolf

Howlin' Wolf is raw Delta fury on a raging bulldozer, gargling acid, roaring nitroglycerin, and decimating recording studio soundboards with undreamed of and uncontainable decibel force: the most menacing, compelling force of smoldering energy ever to explode on stage. One of six children born to Dock Burnett and his wife Gertrude, Chester Arthur Burnett was born on a plantation between West Point and Aberdeen, near Tupelo, Mississippi, on June 10, 1910. A farmer for much of his early life, Burnett moved with his family to Ruleville where he encountered the legendary Charlie Patton c.1928 and became enthralled by the spell of his powerful performances, forging out of Patton's style and the influences of the yodeling/falsetto leaps of Tommy Johnson and white country singer Jimmie Rodgers a nascent style that would grow to legendary proportions later when he recreated himself in the image of the larger-than-life, feral howler who was energy and evil attitude incarnate. Burnett began performing around Mississippi and Arkansas intermittently in the 1930's, but he returned, serendipitously, to farm and family at a time when his sister's beau (and future husband) was Rice Miller, who taught Wolf the rudiments of harmonica that would so enliven his later recordings. After a stint in the Army in 1941-1945 and a bit more farming, Burnett formed a band in 1948, one that complemented his visceral sound with a jazzy, hopped up, manic energy that rocked the joints in the West Memphis area. By 1949 the band was broadcasting over KWEM radio in Memphis, where Burnett also worked as a DJ and producer. Two years later he and his band made their recording debut at Sam Phillips's Memphis Recording Service, with Willie Johnson's guitar, Willie Steele's drums, and occasional piano from Ike Turner matching Wolf howl for howl, producing over the next few years some of the most unadulterated blues ever barely contained on record grooves. Contractual squabbles between Modern and Chess—Wolf had material released simultaneously on both labels—were eventually ironed out, and Wolf moved to Chicago where he put together studio groups that included some of Chicago's premier blues musicians, including Otis Spann, Henry Gray, and Hosea Lee Kennard on piano, Jody Williams and Hubert Sumlin on guitar, and Willie Dixon on bass. In Chicago, Wolf didn't miss a beat, continuing to produce Delta-inflected amplified masterpiece after masterpiece, "Evil Is Going On," "Forty Four," and "Smokestack Lightning" among his immortal recordings from the period. In the late 1950s, under the guidance of Willie Dixon, he produced another collection of triumphant recordings—"Spoonful," "Back Door Man," "I Ain't Superstitious," "Howling for My Darling," "Wang Dang Doodle" were tightly arranged, up to date, contemporary blues classics that featured a 50-year-old Wolf, who nonetheless sounded perfectly comfortable in surrounding somewhat smoother and slicker than his previous recordings, and the bouncy, quivering guitar of Sumlin, who was practically Wolf's adoptive son. After the success of Wolf's *Rockin Chair* LP, he captured the imagination of European audiences sufficiently to tour with the American Folk Blues Festival in 1964, influencing an entire generation of British rockers, who lionized Wolf—the Rolling Stones even arranged for Wolf to appear on the popular rock show *Shindig*, and a group of his disciples recorded a *London Sessions* LP with him in 1970. He continued to tour throughout the 1960s and 1970s to increasing acclaim—he received an honorary Doctor of Arts degree from Columbia College and a Montreux Festival Award for his LP *The Back Door Wolf*—but heart and kidney problems eventually slowed him down, and he died of cancer on January 10, 1976. His presence in both the Blues and Rock and Roll Halls of Fame attest to his influence and popularity. He is one of the immortals of American Music.

Howlin' Wolf

Muddy Waters

If there is one person who best represents the spirit, power, and sound of postwar Chicago blues, transmuting Delta funk into brash, swaggering, amplified glory and formulating the group structure and style that served as the launching pad for many solo careers and launched a million blues bands, it is Muddy Waters. The man who put his birthplace of Rolling Fork, Mississippi, on the map was born McKinley Morganfield on April 4, 1915, one of ten children born to farmer/musician Ollie Morganfield and his wife Bertha Jones. After Bertha's death when Muddy was about three, the family moved to the Stovall-Clarksdale area, where Muddy lived with his grandmother, got some schooling, and worked the farm. As a young man he sang in church choirs, picked up the harmonica from age seven to nine, and taught himself the guitar c.1932, working with a string band or Scott Bohanner at suppers, picnics, and juke joints around Clarksdale and touring briefly with the Silas Green Minstrel Show in 1941. Muddy made his first recording for Alan Lomax of the Library of Congress in 1941-42, producing solos, duets, and string band sides that revealed his archaic Delta roots and his strong, assured adaptations of the music of Son House and Robert Johnson to his own considerable talents. The spark of genius was already there, particularly in the depth of emotion conveyed by Muddy's full-throated, soulful voice. In May 1943, Muddy left Chicago to try his luck and, armed with an electric guitar bought for him by his cousin, he threw himself into the music scene and found encouragement from the reigning giants Big Bill Broonzy and John Lee Williamson. His first commercial recording, "Mean Red Spider" for the 20th Century label, does not quite reflect Muddy's strengths and style, nor do his Columbia sessions from the same year. He formed a band with Jimmy Rogers and Blue Smitty, and later with Baby Face Leroy, but got his real break when Sunnyland Slim took him to Chess Brothers's Aristocrat label in 1947,

beginning a recording association with the Chess Brothers that would stretch all the way to 1975. During that period, as Muddy's true style emerged, he became an undisputed king of Chicago blues. With a voice that could leap from a whisper to a scream, from baritone to soprano falsetto, in a flash, always subtly nuanced with the moan, glissandi, and melisma of a field holler, and charged with a powerful, sensual urgency, Muddy was the master of the field. His whining, deep blues slide guitar, now also drawing from Tampa Red and Robert Nighthawk, could evoke backwoods and big city life on every fret. Additionally, his impeccable choice of band mates helped make his music so influential as well—the nimble, beautifully interweaving guitar of Jimmy Rogers, bass from Big Crawford and Willie Dixon, rippling piano from Otis Spann, and the high number of greats who graced Muddy's harmonica chair, from Little Walter to Big Walter to Junior Wells to George Smith to James Cotton and beyond. Armed with songs of his own creation and tunes from the pen of Willie Dixon, Muddy conquered the blues world with some of the most stunningly powerful blues ever.: "She Moves Me," "Hoochie Coochie Man," "Just Make Love to Me," "I'm Ready," "Got My Mojo Working," "Forty Days and Forty Nights" and so many more. Appearances with Chris Barber in England in 1958, at Carnegie Hall in 1959-1961, and at the Newport Jazz Festival in 1960 helped expose Muddy to new audiences and extend his influence beyond the blues field to virtually every white blues rocker, and he also went on to appear on TV and in movies, experiencing wide success up until his death on April 30, 1983. His numerous awards, from *Downbeat, Billboard, Blues Unlimited, Ebony,* the Grammys, and inductions into the Blues and Rock and Roll Halls of Fame only confirm what anybody who heard him already knew: here was a human voice and human soul pushed to their fullest potential, their greatest expression, generating timeless art without pretension. Whence comes such another?

Muddy Waters

John Lee Hooker

Magnificent despair: nobody conveys the brooding, visceral power of the low-down-Saturday night-gutbucket-awful moanin'-sho nuff black and blue blues as breathtakingly as John Lee Hooker. Hooker drew his first breath on August 22, 1917, in Clarksdale, Mississippi, one of eleven children born to Delta sharecroppers, but by age 14 the smell from behind a plow helped convince him to pack his Delta roots and hit the highway. After stints in Memphis, where he performed with Robert Nighthawk, and Cincinnati, where he sang with gospel groups, Hooker moved to Detroit in 1943, forming a group and playing the small joints of the Detroit Black Bottom ghetto. He began his remarkably prolific recording career with Modern Records in 1948, rising immediately to the top of the "Race" charts with the enduring and oft-re-recorded classic "Boogie Chillen," and over the years has recorded under such names as Birmingham Sam and His Magic Guitar, Texas Slim, John Lee Booker, and John Lee Cooker for well over two dozen labels—JVB, Fortune, Gotham, VeeJay, Specialty, Chess, and King among them. Hooker's broad and enduring attraction stems from his hypnotic sound, mesmerizing at any tempo—frequently a modal energy field across which Hooker fires off scattershot, strangulated missives and shattering chords that seem barely separated, if at all, from the soul that created them—and from a deep-hued, stark voice that is fascinatingly disturbing. Over the years his version of Tony Hollins's "Crawlin' King Snake," and other songs like "House Rent Boogie," "Boom Boom Boom Boom," "I'm in the Mood," "Union Station Blues," "Walkin' the Boogie," "Nightmare Blues," "Whiskey and Wimmen," and "Moanin' Blues" have helped define and revivify the deep blues tradition, first for African American audiences and then, during the "folk revival," for whites in this country and around the world. He has influenced Buddy Guy, Junior Parker, and countless blues performers as well as blues-rock purveyors Steve Miller, the Groundhogs, and Canned Heat, the latter basing a part of their reputation on their reformulations of Hooker's formidable boogie permutations—all of which have served to get him inducted into the Blues and Rock and Roll Halls of Fame. In the 1980s and 1990s Hooker has become an institution, featured on MTV and recording with countless rock superstars eagerly lining up for a chance to boogie with the Hook. Still, the most rewarding setting for his music is still when the man sits down alone, with only his guitar and stomping foot to accompany him, and sings burning hell.

John Lee Hooker
Jack Coughlin

Aleck "Sonny Boy Williamson" Miller

Sonny Boy Williamson is one of the most dynamic and distinctive stylists in all of American music, with a seemingly effortless virtuosity that brilliantly insinuates both slackness and tautness simultaneously and thereby captures a passion that is so sensual that it verges on the spiritually, ecstatically obscene. Born to Millie Ford in Glendora, Mississippi, on December 5, 1897 or 1899, young Aleck took his step-father Jim Miller's surname and was dubbed "Rice" as a child. Teaching himself harmonica at age five, he left home in the early 1920s to hobo and work joints, parties, picnics, and street corners throughout the South, where he met and performed under the name "Little Boy Blue" with Robert Johnson, Big Boy Crudup, Elmore James, and Robert Lockwood. Lockwood joined Miller, now appearing as Sonny Boy Williamson, on the King Biscuit Hour on KFFA radio in Helena, Arkansas, selling flour, promoting upcoming gigs, and spreading their fame throughout the South. Although he insisted that he was the original Sonny Boy, Miller had apparently adopted the monicker of John Lee Williamson to cash in on the recording star's celebrity, though in time Miller would demonstrate forcefully that, with his striking musical personality, the masquerade was unnecessary and even ludicrous. After making a name for himself on radio and in jukes in the 1940s, Miller embarked on a recording career with Lillian McMurry's Trumpet label in 1951, recording over the next few years as leader and astonishing sideman for Arthur Crudup, Bobo Thomas, and Elmore James. After some time in Detroit playing with Baby Boy Warren, he wound up in Chicago recording for Chess Records beginning in 1955. Already an elder statesman and legend, rather than resting on his laurels he proceeded to top his previous recordings with performances that were by turns slyly groping, gently undulating, lunging bursts of climactic hysteria, highly organized but spontaneous-sounding masterpieces. With bands that included Lockwood, Luther Tucker, Matt Murphy, Buddy Guy, Otis Spann, and Lafayette Leake, Miller created masterpiece after masterpiece, "Don't Start Me to Talking," "Your Funeral and My Trial," "Nine Below Zero," "Help Me," and "Decoration Day Blues" demonstrating the worldly wise, direct, and heartfelt emotion that is the bedrock of the blues and ensuring his induction into the Blues Hall of Fame. 1963 found Miller a traveling ambassador of the blues, bowler hat and all, in Europe, inspiring young British blues-rockers like John Mayall and Eric Clapton but perplexing many with his enigmatic personality. At times sly, ornery, charming, and violent, almost a walking exemplification of the blues lyric "you don't know my mind," his behavior likely represented the series of masks he had learned to wear in order to protect himself as an African American in the Jim Crow South. He died on May 25, 1965, in Helena, Arkansas, and remains to this day for many people *the* Sonny Boy, in the words employed in the title to a composition by jazz man Archie Shepp, "The Original Sonny Boy Williamson."

Sonny Boy Williamson — (Rice Miller)

Big Walter Horton

Big Walter Horton did not have the extroverted personality of some of his other harmonica contemporaries, but his brilliant harmonica playing, so adaptable to a variety of formats and styles, epitomized sensitivity, subtlety, and taste. Born in Horn Lake, Mississippi, a bit south of Memphis, on April 6, 1917/1918, young Walter took up harmonica when he was five, moving with his family to Mound City, Arkansas, and then on to Memphis where, unable to do heavy work due to ill health, he took to playing on the streets for the cash he could muster. He claimed to have recorded with the Memphis Jug band in 1927 (he would have been around nine years old!) and with Little Buddy Doyle in 1939—and certainly he had been a familiar presence on the Memphis music scene on the streets, at jukes, at parties, and at W.C. Handy Park, frequently in the company of Floyd Jones and Honeyboy Edwards—but his first confirmed recordings were made at Sam Phillips's Memphis Recording Service at 706 Union Avenue in Memphis for Modern/RPM in 1951. This place where so many blues, R&B, and rock and roll artists got their start—including B.B.King, Howlin' Wolf, Bobby Bland, and Elvis Presley—recorded Horton in the company of Joe Hill Louis, Willie Johnson, Jimmy DeBerry, and Calvin and Phineas Newborn, producing recordings from 1951-1953 that show a Horton already fully conversant with the harmonica, nearly arrived at his mature style, and pumping up his recordings and those done as a sideman with spirited harp work on everything from rough country boogies like "Blues in the Morning" to moseying-along lopers like "Easy" to shattering small combo electric blues like "Black Gal." However, in 1953 Horton was off to Chicago to work with Johnny Shines and Muddy Waters, recording some classic sides with Shines for JOB, including the amazing "Evening Sun," some sides with his own band for States in 1954, and work for Chess and Cobra with Muddy/Jimmy Rogers and Otis Rush in the mid to late 1950s. By the mid 1960s he was tapped by blues revivalists to appear on various European tours that cemented his reputation and led to extensive recordings on Decca, Fontana, Arhoolie, Vanguard, and many other labels, including accompaniments to Floyd Jones, Willie Dixon, Johnny Young, Johnny Shines, and Johnny Winter. Horton's mature style demonstrated his consummate abilities as a soloist and accompanist, capable of producing an impressive variety of effects and sounds: deliberate, single-note patterns, warm double-note blends, staccato, boxy echoes, shrill piglet squeals, and some of the tenderest fluttering this side of a cooing mourning dove, the various elements coalescing into brilliantly logical, unified, touching solos. Horton continued to record and tour throughout the 1960s and 1970s, recording most importantly with his protege, Carey Bell, for Alligator in 1972 (and producing the indescribably beautiful masterpiece "Trouble in Mind") and with Muddy for Blue Sky in 1977, which increased his visibility and fame. When he died on December 8, 1981, he was mourned as a true harp master with a sound and style that was his alone and recognized officially through his induction into the Blues Hall of Fame. Saddled with a number of distasteful nicknames in his life, it is best to remember him simply as "Big Walter," big as in talent, heart, and soul.

Walter Horton

Joe Hill Louis

A prime contender for heavyweight champion of one man bands is Joe Hill Louis, whose brilliant and spirited coordination of vocals, guitar, harmonica, high hat, and traps, and his versatility and breadth as a session musician, produced some of the most downhome music to reach release during the 1940s and 1950s. Born Leslie (or Lester) Hill in the Froggy Bottom section near Whitehaven, Tennessee, on September 23, 1921, Hill lost his mother and endured frequent beatings at the hands of his stepmother until the age of 14, when he ran away to Memphis and became a house servant for the well-to-do Canale family. He was dubbed Joe Hill Louis after the famous boxer when he bested a local tough guy in a boxing match, a colorful nickname that stuck with him the rest of this life, even when his ebullient personality earned him the handle of "The BeBop Boy." He graduated from Jew's harp to harmonica in his formative musical years, then added guitar and percussion to his act as a way to eliminate having to share performance fees with other band members, drawing the jealousy of other less versatile musicians. Appearances in jukes, clubs, at Handy Park, and on street corners spread his name enough to land him the job as replacement for B.B.King advertising Pepticon on WDIA radio in Memphis. By the time he first recorded for Columbia in 1949, all the elements of his mature style were in place. Learning directly from Memphis jug band performers Will Shade and Dewey Corley, he nonetheless also absorbed the harmonica influences of both Sonny Boy Williamsons and the boogie guitar beat of John Lee Hooker, as well as the blaring, unrestrained single-string style of the guitarists of the West Memphis blues scene. As a result, Louis was remarkably adaptable, switching from the churning sound of "Boogie in the Park" to the rough country sound of "Big Legged Woman" to the menacing urban edge of "When I Am Gone" with ease. During his career he saw releases on Columbia, Modern, Meteor, Checker, Sun, Rockin', and other labels, working as a leader and as sideman to artists such as Jack Kelly, Billy Love, Walter Horton, and Rufus Thomas. Louis died on August 5, 1957, having contracted tetanus from a cut infected by fertilizer he was using in yard work, cutting short a career that certainly would have thrived in the time of the coming blues revival, and cheating us of more wild and wonderful sounds from the colorful Be-Bop boy.

Joe Hill Louis

Jack Coughlin

Little Walter

There has been no more visionary and inventive instrumentalist in the blues tradition, and no one who more effectively communicated those qualities with more virtuosity and passion, than Marion "Little Walter" Jacobs. Born to Adam Jacobs and Beatrice Leviege in Marksville, Louisiana, on May 1, 1930, the future Blues Hall of Famer taught himself to play harmonica at age eight, playing on the streets and in clubs throughout the South until he settled in Chicago c.1946, where the tips on Maxwell Street, occasional work with Tampa Red, Big Bill Broonzy, and Memphis Slim, and the chance to see his major influence, John Lee "Sonny Boy" Williamson, kept him hustling and striving firmly on the path to formulating the style that would revolutionize harmonica technique and aesthetics. Recordings for Ora Nelle, Tempo-Tone, and Parkway/Regal in 1947-1950 produced some wonderful sides in Walter's early, neo-Sonny Boy style, but it was his recordings on Chess Records with Muddy Waters beginning in 1950, especially his performance on "Country Boy" from 1951, that featured the heavily amplified style that first proclaimed on record the emergence of a potent new force on the blues horizon. In 1952, his instrumental hit "Juke" confirmed his promise and initiated a string of artistic and/or commercial triumphs as Little Walter and His Night Cats, or Little Walter and His Jukes, on Chess Records—15 chart successes between 1952 and 1959, and a sometimes grueling touring schedule. Stylistically, it wasn't that Walter was the first to use the amplified technique with his harmonica. But he was the first to envision the potential of this new technique and harness the power of this new galaxy of sounds, to see beyond superficial volume to the aesthetic possibilities for color, tone, tension, and force. To him, the amplified harmonica was a new instrument with unexplored, unmined potential, and he proceeded to blast away at the boundaries with such avant garde aspiration that over forty years later listeners are still wondering not only how he did what he did technically but also how he ever conceived of his innovations. Clearly both Sonny Boy and Big Walter were influences, as were Louis Jordan and bop saxophonists, but no rehearsal of influences can account for the drive, the swing, the nuance, the imagination, the subtle adaptation of sound to mood, the unparalleled experimentation with harmonica "positions" and the chromatic harmonica in blues that burst forth in Walter's relatively brief performing career. Combined with a sincere and affecting singing voice—John Lee Hooker called Walter his favorite singer—and a penchant for tight arrangements executed by highly proficient, jazz-influenced musicians, he produced a body of work that is truly awe-inspiring, both under his own name and as accompanist to Waters, Jimmy Rogers, John Brim, Bo Diddley, and others. When he died as a result of a street scuffle on February 15, 1968, a victim of the stormy and violent life he lived, his powers were clearly waning, but few blues harmonica players since his emergence have gone uninfluenced by him, and most have been heavily influenced by his oeuvre. Testimony to his dominance of the field is the fact that no blues harmonica player since Walter has emerged with any significant advancement on his work or radical re-envisioning of the harmonica's role or possibilities, though he has had his talented disciples, and harmonica innovators in non-blues fields frequently acknowledge his continuing inspiration and influence.

Little Walter

Jack Coughlin

George Smith

Anyone who questions whether the blues has anything to do with Birmingham's bombs or Montgomery's bus boycotts or Little Rock's Guard-force racism needs only listen to nearly five minutes of soul-drenched grits and gravy blues entitled "Blues for Reverend King" to hear all the anguish of Jim Crow buses, segregated lunch counters, and high school battle grounds distilled into one mighty and imperial tribute to a symbol of the struggle for equal rights. It is an astonishing tour through the emotional landscape of African Americans, by turns wistful, raging, and soothing but strong-willed and determined, the supreme musical moment in a career of many highlights of one of the dominant post-Little Walter harmonica stylists, George "Harmonica" Smith. He was born Allen George Smith in Helena, Arkansas, on April 22, 1924, one of three children of George Smith, Sr., and his wife, Jessie. Taught to play harmonica at age four by his musically talented mother, Smith performed around the area of his home in Cairo, Illinois, in the mid-1930s and was featured in Earley Wood's Country Band, touring Mississippi, Kentucky, Illinois, and elsewhere as soon as he was old enough to hobo. After stints in Illinois and Mississippi, where Smith was one of the first harmonica players to experiment with amplification, Smith landed in Chicago c. 1949, at first working outside of music but ultimately playing with Otis Rush and touring the South with Muddy Waters. In 1954, Smith landed a steady gig at the Orchid Room in Kansas City, where he was spotted and signed in 1955 by Modern Records' Joe Bihari, who swept him into a KC studio to produce two enduring Smith classics, "Telephone Blues" and "Blues in the Dark." On his 1955-56 Modern sides Smith reveals a distinctive, mature harmonica style that draws Larry Adler and Little Walter but imitates neither, wielding the chromatic as his instrument of choice and foregrounding smooth riffing and powerful octave runs mixed with swooping and heartfelt passages that are powerfully direct. Vocally, Smith was also direct and passionate, singing in an unadorned style most frequently, though his yodeling passages in "Hey Mr. Porter" are an interesting exception. 1955 found Smith providing gentle, relaxed playing behind Jack Dupree at Cincinnati's King Record studios, just one of a number of brilliant cameo appearances that demonstrates Smith's adaptability. That year Smith settled in Los Angeles, basing there for the rest of his life and recording as Little Walter, Jr., the Harmonica King, and George Allen for a variety of labels—Lapel, J&M, Caddy, Sotoplay, and Carolyn among them. A reunion with Muddy in 1966, recorded for Spivey Records, revived his career and brought him a new White audience, resulting in two excellent but very different LPs: *Blues With a Feeling* on World Pacific, a wonderful tribute to Little Walter that showed what Smith could do in a Chicago blues band setting, and *...of the Blues* on Bluesway, which stretched both harmonica and blues boundaries by encompassing material from "Got My Mojo Working" to bluesy versions of "Ode to Billie Joe" and "Hawaiian Eye." Through these and subsequent LPs on Blue Horizon, BluesTime, Deram, and other labels, including marvelous accompaniments to Sunnyland Slim on World Pacific and to Joe Turner, T-Bone Walker, and Otis Spann on the *Super Black Blues* LP, Smith influenced an entire generation of harp players, especially West Coast players lucky enough to experience his performing and generosity firsthand. He continued to tour and record throughout the 1970s and early 1980s, and though he was slowed down by a series of heart attacks, he produced one last album for Murray Brothers before he died of a heart attack on October 1, 1983.

George Smith

Jack Coughlin '97

James Cotton

Superharp, they call him, and it is a label that fits James Cotton's turbo-charged harmonica style perfectly. From his birth in Tunica, Mississippi, on July 1, 1935, Cotton began soaking up the rich sounds of the Delta region, working on a farm, singing in church choirs, and falling in love with the sounds of harmonica whiz "Rice" Miller that he heard on the radio when he was only seven. When Cotton was around 10 he ran away from home to work with Miller, appearing occasionally on King Biscuit Time on KFFA and working with Howlin' Wolf and Willie Nix in West Memphis. After recording with Wolf, he cut four sides of his own for Sun Records in 1954, including his classic "Cotton Crop Blues" with Auburn Hare on guitar. That same year he replaced Junior Wells (who himself had replaced Little Walter) in the coveted harmonica spot in Muddy Waters's band, remaining for some 12 years and benefitting from the increasingly national and international exposure brought about by the "blues revival," particularly for those talented enough to back someone of Muddy's stature. Besides recording with Waters, Cotton cut some sides of his own in Chicago and some EPs in England, in addition to stellar, blasting accompaniments to Otis Spann, but after he was featured as a leader in Vanguard's *Chicago/The Blues/Today* series, featuring a hard-hitting remake of "Cotton Crop," a wild "Rocket 88," and a desolate "The Blues Keep Fallin'," Cotton was clearly about to become a major force. What followed for the Verve label were three LPs, two of them at the top of the list of best blues recordings of the 1960s. Cotton's power, deep blues feeling, and versatility stunned and enthralled blues fans and blues-rock admirers like Mike Bloomfield and Paul Butterfield who had gathered about him to learn, and they lent assistance, through their blues-rock circuit connections, to the emerging star. The recordings mixed downhome blues, Chicago blues, uptown blues, and R &B/soul, all played impeccably by one of the premier working blues bands of the day, with the amazing flutter-picking of Luther Tucker, virtuoso piano of Alberto Gianquinto, and crack rhythm section of Bob Anderson and Sam Lay, supplemented by sympathetic, charging horn charts. But the real star was Cotton, with his powerful, grainy voice and blasting harmonica played with threatening abandon. Songs like "Blues in My Sleep," and "The Creeper" are over-the-top masterpieces that demonstrate Cotton's willingness to confront the limit's of amplification and attack with a raw force that is nearly overwhelming—though of course he could blow a more restrained, subtle blues on songs like "Down at Your Buryin'." Although these recordings are the high water mark of Cotton's career, he continued to produce top-notch recordings as leader and sideman for Chess, Capitol, Buddah, Jackal, Antone's, and Alligator before reuniting with Verve Records in the 1990s. His live shows are filled with harmonica fireworks and tight arrangements that place his act still among the best in blues, and he continues to inspire harmonica players as he did in the early days when he was heir apparent to Little Walter's harmonica throne.

George Smith
Jack Coughlin '97

James Cotton
Jack Coughlin

Selected Discography/ Videography

JOHN HENRY BARBEE
Blues Master Vol. 3, Storyville CD 8003.
Memphis Blues (1927-1938), Document DOCD 5159 (Barbee's five pre-war cuts are included).

BIG BILL BROONZY
Big Bill Broonzy: Complete Recorded Works in Chronological Order, 1927-1947, Document DOCD 5050-5052; 5126-5133; 6047 (12 CDs).
Big Bill Broonzy Sings Folk Songs, Smithsonian Folkways CD 40023.
Blues in the Mississippi Night, Rykodisc RCD 90155.

The Blues, VIDJAZZ 13, contains video of three songs by Broonzy; *Legends of Country Blues Guitar*, Vestapol 13003, contains video of four more songs by Broonzy.

JAMES COTTON
Best of the Verve Years, Verve CD 314 527 371-2.
Chicago/The Blues/Today! Vol.2, Vanguard CD 79217.
Live From Chicago--Mr. Superharp Himself, Alligator CD 4746.

WILLIE DIXON
The Big Three Trio, Columbia CD CT 46216.
The Original Wang Dang Doodle, Chess CD CHC 9353.
Willie's Blues, Original Blues Classics CD 501.

Maintenance Shop Blues, Yazoo Video 511, consists of a video of Dixon and his group.

CHAMPION JACK DUPREE
Blues from the Gutter, Atlantic CD 7 82434-2.
Champion Jack Dupree Sings the Blues, King CD - 735.
New Orleans Barrelhouse Piano, Columbia CD CK 52834-2.

BLIND BOY FULLER
Blind Boy Fuller: Complete Recorded Works in Chronological Order, Document DOCD 5091-5096 (6 CDs)

BILLIE HOLIDAY
Billie's Blues, Blue Note CDP 7 48786 2.
The Complete Billie Holiday on Verve, Verve 314 517 658-2.
The Lady: Billie Holiday Complete Collection, CBS Sony CD OODP 570-577 (8CDs).

Billie Holiday: The Many Faces of Lady Day is a 60 minute documentary dealing with Holiday's life.

JOHN LEE HOOKER
Graveyard Blues, Specialty CD 7018.
Half a Stranger, Mainstream CD 903.
House of the Blues, MCA CD 9258.
The Legendary Modern Recordings, Flair CD 39658
The Ultimate Collection: 1948-1990, Rhino 2 CD 70572.

Vestapol Video 13035 contains 60 minutes of videos of Hooker in a variety of settings.

BIG WALTER HORTON
Big Walter Horton, Alligator CD 4702.
Mouth Harp Maestro, Flair CD 86297.

SON HOUSE
Son House and the Great Delta Blues Singers, Document DOCD 5002.
Son House: The Complete Library of Congress Recordings, Travelin' Man CD 02.
Son House: Father of the Delta Blues, Columbia CD C2K 48867.

Bukka White and Son House, Yazoo Video 500 (9 cuts by House).
Legends of the Delta Blues, Vestapol Video 13038 (5 cuts by House).
Legends of Bottleneck Blues Guitar, Vestapol Video 13002, contains video of two songs by House; *Legends of Country Blues Guitar Vol. 1*, Vestapol Video 13003, contains video of two songs by House; *Legends of Country Blues Guitar Vol. 2*, Vestapol Video 13016, contains video of one song by House; *Devil Got My Woman*, Vestapol Video 13049, contains video of recordings by House at the 1964 Newport Festival.

BLIND LEMON JEFFERSON
Complete Recorded Works in Chronological Order, Document DOCD 5017-5020 (4 CDs).
King of the Country Blues, Yazoo CD 1069.

ROBERT JOHNSON
Robert Johnson: The Complete Recordings, 2 CD 46222.

JOE HILL LOUIS
The Be-Bop Boy with Walter Horton and Mose Vinson, Bear Family BCD 15524.

BIG MACEO
Big Maceo: The King of Chicago Blues Piano, Arhoolie CD 7009.
Charlie Spand/Big Maceo, Old Tramp OTCD 04.

ALECK "SONNY BOY WILLIAMSON" MILLER
Clownin' With the World, Acoustic Archives CD 700 (plus recordings by Willie Love).
Goin' In Your Direction, Acoustic Archives CD 801 (as leader and with Crudup and Thomas).
King Biscuit Time, Arhoolie CD 310.
Sonny Boy Williamson: The Chess Years, Charly CD Red Box 1.

The Blues, VIDJAZZ 13 features video of three songs by Sonny Boy taped in Copenhagen in 1963.

MEMPHIS MINNIE
Hoodoo Lady 1933-1937, Columbia CD CK 46775.
I Ain't No Bad Gal, Portrait RK 44072.
Memphis Minnie and Kansas Joe Vols. 1-4, Document DOCD 5028-5031. (4 CDs).
Memphis Minnie: Complete Recorded Works 1935-41, RST BDCD 6008-6012 (5 CDs).
Memphis Minnie: Complete Postwar Recordings, Wolf WBCD 008-010 (3 CDs).

MA RAINEY
Ma Rainey's Black Bottom, Yazoo CD 1071.
The Paramounts Chronologically Vol. 1, Black Swan HCD 12001.
The Paramounts Chronologically Vol. 2, Black Swan HCD 12002.
The Paramounts Chronologically Vol. 5, Black Swan HCD 12005.

MEMPHIS SLIM
Alone with My Friends, Original Blues Classics CD 581.
The Complete Recordings 1940-1941, Blues Collection CD 158 032.
The Real Folk Blues, Chess CD 9270.
Together Again One More Time/Still Not Ready for Eddie, Antone's CD 0305.

BESSIE SMITH
Bessie Smith: The Complete Recordings Volumes 1-5, Columbia CD 47091 / 47471 / 47474 / 52838 / 57546.

The Blues, VIDJAZZ 13, includes the "St. Louis Blues" film short in which Smith appears.

GEORGE SMITH
Blues With a Feeling, World Pacific LP-21887.
Harmonica Ace, Flair CD V2-86298.
...of the Blues, Bluesway LP BLS 6029.

ROOSEVELT SYKES
Complete Recorded Works in Chronological Order, 1929-1944, Document CD 5116-5122 (7 CDs).
Hard Drivin' Blues, Delmark CD-607.

Big Bill Broonzy/Roosevelt Sykes, Yazoo Video #518, features video performances of each of these artists performing separately.

SONNY TERRY
Back to New Orleans, Fantasy 24708.
Sonny Terry: Complete Recordings 1938-1945 in Chronological Order, Document DOCD 5230.
Whoopin' the Blues: The Capitol Recordings 1947-1950, Capitol 29372.

The Blues, VIDJAZZ 13, contains one video selection featuring Sonny Terry, and he also appears in *Out of the Blacks, Into the Blues*, Yazoo 506 and 507. Vestapol Videos 13056/13057/13060 are devoted to videos of Sonny Terry and Brownie McGhee.

LITTLE WALTER
The Blues World of Little Walter, Delmark DD-648.
Little Walter: The Chess Years 1952-1963, Charly CD Red Box 5.

MUDDY WATERS
The Best of Muddy Waters, Chess CHD 31268
The Complete Muddy Waters, 1947-1967, Charly CD Red Box 3.
The Complete Plantation Recordings, Chess CD 9344.

Maintenance Shop Blues, Yazoo Video 506, contains video of Muddy performing with his band.

JOHN LEE "SONNY BOY" WILLIAMSON
Sonny Boy Williamson: Complete Recording Works in Chronological Order, Document 5055-5059 (5 CDs) (These titles are also being reissued in the American RCA Bluebird Series, starting with RCA 07863 66723-2.)

HOWLIN' WOLF
Howlin' Wolf: The Complete Recordings 1951-1969, Charly CD Red Box 7.
Howlin' Wolf Rides Again, Flair CD V-2-86295.

Devil Got My Woman, Vestapol 13049, contains video of three recordings by Howlin' Wolf.